HOW TO TELL A
SECRET

Also by P.J. Huff & J.G. Lewin

How to Feed an Army: Recipes and Lore from the Front Lines

Witness to the Civil War: First-Hand Accounts from
Frank Leslie's Illustrated Newspaper

HOW TO TELL A SECRET

TIPS, TRICKS & TECHNIQUES FOR BREAKING CODES & CONVEYING COVERT INFORMATION

P.J. Huff & J.G. Lewin

Collins
An Imprint of HarperCollinsPublishers

HarperCollins books may be purchased for educational, business, or sales promotional use. For information, please write: Special Markets Department, HarperCollins Publishers, 10 East 53rd Street, New York, NY 10022.

FIRST EDITION

Designed by Nicola Ferguson

Printed on acid-free paper

Library of Congress Cataloging-in-Publication Data

Huff, P. J.
    How to tell a secret : tips, tricks, and techniques for breaking codes and conveying covert information / P.J. Huff & J.G. Lewin.
      p. cm.
    Includes bibliographical references and index.
    ISBN: 978-0-06-113794-5
    ISBN-10: 0-06-113794-4
    1. Defense information, Classified—United States—Popular works. 2. Confidential communications—United States—History—Popular works. 3. Ciphers—History—Popular works. 4. Official secrets—United States—Popular works. 5. Undercover operations—United States—History—Popular works. I. Lewin, J. G. II. Title.

UB247.H84 2007
327.12—dc22

                                    2006053036

07 08 09 10 11 WBC/RRD 10 9 8 7 6 5 4 3 2 1

CONTENTS

INTRODUCTION

TELLING A SECRET IS AN ANCIENT AND honorable pastime. (There are those, of course, who would say that keeping a secret is even more honorable, but that's another story.)

There are many ways of telling a secret. It can be whispered into the ear of a friend. It can be written in invisible ink. It can be broadcast over a radio frequency. It can be reduced to the size of the period at the end of this sentence. It can be encrypted in multiple layers of ciphers. It can be buried in a hole in the ground. It can be buried in the code on your desktop computer. It can be scrawled in chalk on the back of a fence post. It can be as lonely as a train whistle. It can be as public as a nationally televised football game.

CAN YOU KEEP A SECRET ?

As long as people have been communicating with one another, there have been secrets. And for nearly as long, we've been finding a way to tell secrets—to the few we deem worthy of the information. Not coincidentally, while all this secret telling has been going on, there have been nearly as many attempts to uncover the secrets of others. It's important. It could help win the game. It could help win the war.

As civilization has progressed, the ways in which we tell a secret have kept pace. The encryption algorithms have become more complicated. The hiding places have become more ingenious. The meanings have become more obscure. And still, someone is out there watching what you're doing and searching for ways to penetrate your secrets.

The problem with secret telling has always been how to convey the message to the right person without the wrong person finding out.

The solutions have been many.

Reading this book will not necessarily make you the neighborhood version of one of the wizards of Bletchley Park (the folks who broke the German ciphers during World War II); that is not our intention. Rather, you will walk away from this book with a fuller appreciation of the complexities involved and the skills required to convey secrets at various times in history as well as in our high-tech age. Examples from the real world will show how it has been done and provide insights into how it continues to be done by the professionals.

The casual observer might well assume that the realms of secret and hidden communications were the exclusive domain of governmental bodies—the military, diplomatic, and intelligence services. But such is not the case. In the early twenty-first century, there are many who have secrets: bankers (with their PINs, or personal identification numbers), computer users (with their passwords), professional sports teams (with their signals from the bench), underground subcultures (with their graffiti scrawled on vacant buildings and highway overpasses), and even superheroes (with their decoder rings and badges). Secrets abound in this world. Telling secrets is not necessarily a nefarious activity; keeping secrets is not necessarily always the right thing to do.

We've attempted here to provide a snapshot of the basic tools you will need in the telling of your secrets: the codes, the ciphers, and the steganography; the signals and mechanical devices; the encryption schemes and computer technologies; the deception and misdirection; and the stuff of spies. And through historical accounts, we'll look at some of the ways these tools have been used and the people who have used them throughout history. There have been glorious successes and magnificent failures.

You may find some of these stories familiar, and many of the names you will have heard before. But the context may be different. You will read about General George Washington as spymaster, how President George Washington was spied on by members of his cabinet, about the real role of magicians among the ancients, and the role of magicians during World War II.

All things are not necessarily as they first appear. It is a secret world out there. Many of those secrets pass before your eyes every day. Heed the words offered by Sherlock Holmes in *A Scandal in Bohemia*: "You see but you do not observe. The distinction is clear."

HOW TO TELL A SECRET

CHAPTER 1

A Cipher Primer

July 1943

THE DAYS WERE HOT IN THE DESERT OF NORTH AFRICA. THE SUN beat down without mercy or discrimination, on man and beast and material. Those clad in olive drab and heavy leggings were simply miserable. Those tiny, nearly invisible creatures of the desert, chiggers and gnats, were out for blood. Jeeps and helmets—and tempers—were hot. It wasn't going to take much to set things off in a bad direction.

Some comfort was to be found in the knowledge that Field Marshal Erwin Rommel's feared Afrika Korps had finally been defeated. A long campaign led by a British attack across the sand dunes and an amphibious invasion, known as Operation Torch, by combined Allied forces into French Morocco, had trapped and destroyed the Italian and German armies, defeating fascism.

Newspaper and radio correspondents in the theater of operations, lacking any solid war news to report now that there was a lull on the battlefield, began to speculate about when and where the next strike would take place. Some said the Middle East; others said the southern coast of France ("the soft underbelly of Europe," as Winston Churchill would call it); still others hinted at Corsica, Sardinia, or Sicily.

This speculation caused a number of problems. First of all, some of it was fairly accurate. It was no secret, of course, that a number of Allied armies were in North Africa, just across the Mediterranean from occupied Europe and the bulk of Axis forces. Nor was it a secret that the Allies would not long remain idle. What was a secret was when and where they would go next.

And all this guesswork was getting in the way of the military's carefully crafted program of disinformation. Great pains were being taken to lure the gaze of Axis analysts away from Sicily. The disinformation campaign was deemed vital, and a major operation was under way to ensure that the misdirection was being applied in ways that would draw no attention to itself. The German secret military intelligence service, the Abwehr, was very good, and not to be underestimated. It was watching carefully for Allied tricks. The journalists' speculations were hampering the flow of disinformation; indeed, they were coming close to countering the program. All this talk of Sicily and soft underbellies and such might have been good for morale on the British and American home fronts, but it was creating havoc for

Dwight D. Eisenhower

The man knew how to keep, and tell, a secret.
(National Archives and Records Administration)

the censors and planners and the skilled practitioners of disinformation. The speculation had to stop. Secrecy and surprise had priority over promoting warm feelings at home.

General Dwight David "Ike" Eisenhower, supreme commander of the Allied forces, was aware of how easily the element of surprise in battle could be lost by the lethal combination of good intentions and ignorance. Some months before, just such a combination had completely blown a successful intelligence operation.

In neutral Portugal, that hotbed of spies and counterspies during the course of the entire war, the Allies' military intelligence group had successfully tapped into the Lisbon offices of the German embassy. The German codes had been successfully penetrated, and Allied cryptologists were listening to conversations taking place within the walls of the embassy itself and reading the messages flying between the embassy and Berlin. In the days before Ultra-based intelligence (see Chapter 4, "The Devices of Secrecy"), it was one of very few fonts of invaluable information, one the Allies had relied on for solid intelligence.

Enter the OSS (the Office of Strategic Services, precursor to today's Central Intelligence Agency, or CIA). Unaware that the embassy had already been co-opted, they mounted an operation of their own. Breaking into the embassy late one night, OSS officers managed to steal the already-stolen codes and place their own listening devices. Unfortunately for everyone (except the Axis powers), the Abwehr discovered the OSS operation. Being pretty good at the game themselves, the Abwehr changed everything in the embassy: the codes, the communication routines, the entire system. Not only did this nullify the OSS operation but it also shut down the Allied military intelligence operation. It was, quite simply, a fiasco.

There was too much riding on the coming Operation Husky to chance another disaster of that scale.

So in a radical and dramatic move, and one that wasn't anticipated by his staff, Eisenhower himself stepped in and took the action required to end all the speculation. He did it quickly and easily in one 15-minute session by calling all the journalists together for a briefing.

He mounted a stage and opened a curtain behind him to display a wall-sized map of Sicily. He said, in effect, here's what we're going to do and here's how we're going to do it. He then proceeded to outline Operation Husky, as the planned invasion of Sicily was known. In this very public setting, he revealed the dates, the times, and the order of battle.

When he had completed his presentation, there was absolute silence in the room. Eisenhower then pointed out to the reporters that everything he had told them was top secret and that the fate of the invasion, the lives of the troops and, perhaps, the outcome of the war, was now contained in their notebooks. He told them that if they chose to continue their speculations or if they chose to spread the word, they themselves would be responsible. Then he left the stage without taking questions.

It has been reported that during the weeks between that briefing and the invasion, not one of the reporters present ever went anywhere alone. They apparently did not discuss the briefing, even among themselves, for fear of being overheard. And it might have been the longest sustained period of restraint in the annals of journalism.

But the speculation stopped. The secret did not leak. Operation Husky took place, exactly as Eisenhower had outlined. Ignorance had been eliminated; secrecy and surprise had been achieved.

By this one act, Ike proved himself to be one of the all-time great secret-tellers. And he showed that the trick isn't necessarily to keep a secret to yourself forever. The real trick is knowing how and when to tell a secret.

ELEMENTS OF SECRET-TELLING

At the risk of expounding upon the obvious, there are two elemental components in the telling of a secret: the "telling" part and the "secret" part.

In the telling, primacy is given to the method(s) employed. The mode of communication need not necessarily be clandestine in order for the secret to be conveyed.

For example, few things are more public than a quick note scrawled on a postcard. Anyone, from the mail carrier to the kids to a houseguest, is liable to take a quick look. But the real message may not be in the scrawled handwriting ("Wish yew here were"). The real message may be hidden, contained in the seemingly

CRYPTOLOGY

From the Greek *kryptos*, meaning "hidden," and *ology*, meaning "the science of," the term *cryptology* encompasses both the science of encoding knowledge and its coun- terscience of decoding the same knowledge. It is a bit of a para- dox, for without one, there would be no need of the other.

sloppy misspelling of *you* (a cipher), or perhaps in the precise words of the phrase *here were* (a code). If the real message is not readily apparent to the casual observer but rather is hidden or disguised in some way, then the telling of the secret is, in itself, secret. That's an important point, one essential to the understanding of the methodologies involved. These methodologies are legion, but they fall into two broad categories: ciphers and codes.

The second part, the secret part, is at least as important as the telling part. It comes down to this: If you must tell a secret, it is best to conceal the fact that the telling is going on in the first place.

The magician on the stage would have his audience believe that his assistant is there to provide him with props and to take away his cape and hat and gloves. Not so. His assistant, usually a woman clad in sequins and glitter with a feather on her head, is there to draw the audience's attention away from the magician. While she may be bending and turning and prancing around, he will be getting ready for his next trick by stuffing a rabbit up his sleeve. Everyone knows that it is not physically possible to create a rabbit out of thin air. And yet the magician seems to do it, and although everyone seems to be watching him the whole time, no one is quite sure how he does it. The assistant is the smoke-and-mirrors part of the act. By her actions, she is performing an essential bit of misdirection. Important things are happening in the magician's sleeve while the audience is watching the assistant. The real magic happening onstage is going on in plain sight, but not in what the magician is doing.

The magic lies in the ways the assistant keeps attention off the magician. They are a team; when she's completed her part and is dancing off the stage, he's ready to begin conjuring the rabbit. And that's the lesson to be learned: how to hide the essential actions in one place while the audience is looking someplace else.

CIPHERS

Stating a message in clear and precise language that everyone can understand, whether written or verbal, is called *plaintext*. Unless you find yourself in a situation with a unique set of circumstances, as did Eisenhower in North Africa, it is not a good idea to use plaintext for secret messages. Plaintext messages can be easily intercepted.

This book is written in plaintext (at least, so we would have you believe). In theory, anyone who can translate the markings on the page into words—that is, anyone with the ability to decipher the letters of the alphabet, should be able to understand the basic premise and get the message presented here. No confusion or secrecy is intended.

If, on the other hand, you were to see

xtercesxaxlletxotxwohx

you might be momentarily confused. The string of letters appears

WINSTON CHURCHILL

Winston Churchill was never at a loss for words. *(Library of Congress)*

In wartime, truth is so precious that she should always be attended by a bodyguard of lies.

Winston Churchill, as quoted by Thomas Griffith in "Ducking the Truth," *Time*, December 24, 1984

to be gibberish. Perhaps the letter placement is not quite random (you do see one character appear more often than others); still, at first glance, it doesn't make much sense. Obviously, this is no longer plaintext. This is *ciphertext.*

Ciphertext is a message that is intentionally difficult to discern. It can be written or verbal. It may use a traditional alphabet; it may use an archaic alphabet (such as ogham or runes). It doesn't have to use an alphabet at all; it may be composed of a series of symbols (hieroglyphics, for example) or numbers. Or some other combination altogether.

Let us assume that you believe that our string of ciphertext is not gibberish. These are not random marks upon the page. Your intelligence sources have given you reason to believe that there was a message hidden here.

Now what?

In this particular instance, the line appears to be a simple *cipher.*

A cipher is a way of encrypting text, indeed, any way of encrypting text. In other words, a cipher scrambles (encrypts) the text in such a way as to hide the meaning from those who aren't supposed to read the message. The more sophisticated the encryption technique, the more difficult the cipher to read.

THE LONE RANGER'S SECRET VICTORY CODE . . . .

"V" for Victory is the most important letter in the alphabet for patriotic Americans, so the Lone Ranger's secret Victory code alphabet starts with "V", to stand for "A", and continues as shown below.

1.	A	B	C	D	E	F	G	H	I	J	K	L	M
2.	V	W	X	Y	Z	A	B	C	D	E	F	G	H
1.	N	O	P	Q	R	S	T	U	V	W	X	Y	Z
2.	I	J	K	L	M	N	O	P	Q	R	S	T	U

To write a message in this secret Victory code, use the letters in line 2 in place of the ones immediately above in the regular alphabet in line 1, using V for A, W for B, and so on. Thus you would write BOY as WJT. When you receive a message written in the Lone Ranger's secret Victory Code, write down in place of each letter the one that appears directly above it in line 1. Thus QDXOJMT deciphers to read VICTORY.
Copyright, 1943, The Lone Ranger, Inc.

Lone Ranger code card

If your parents bought the right brand of bread, you'd have access to the Lone Ranger's Secret Victory Code. The trick was to get the other guy's parents to buy the same brand of bread. Technically, this isn't a code. It is, rather, the key to a simple substitution cipher. (Hake's Americana)

There are a number of ways to encrypt a message. One of the earlier forms is a *substitution cipher,* in which the letters are scrambled so that one letter stands for another.

Consider the Lone Ranger's cipher. During the 1940s and 1950s, the "masked man of the plains" was at the peak of his popularity and starred in radio, movies, books, and comics. Sponsors would ride along with the popularity and offer premiums to their customers, often emblazoned with the Lone Ranger's likeness. (Today all this is called a tie-in). One such premium was the card pictured here.

Distributed during the height of World War II, this card detailed the Lone Ranger's substitution cipher. Using this card, a message could be encrypted quickly by substituting one letter of the alphabet for another.

Thus, the message

meeting tonight

would read

hzzodib ojidbco

Fairly simple, but without the *key*, it is indecipherable.

The key is the element that will allow you to unlock the cipher. It is the tool that, when applied, gives you the insight to decipher the message, to translate it from ciphertext to plaintext. In this instance, the Lone Ranger card itself is the key. For it to be most effective, both the sender and the receiver of this message would have the key (that is, their parents would have to buy the same brand of bread).

But this key won't work with our sample message above, so there's something else going on there.

There are two major categories of ciphers. The first, as we've just seen, is the substitution cipher; the second is the *transposition cipher*.

A transposition cipher moves the original text into a different order, rearranging individual letters or entire words, sometimes adding characters to add to the obfuscation.

One common form of transposition cipher is the anagram. This is a word game in which letters of one word are switched around to form another word. (An anagram of *Elvis*, for example, is *Lives*. All the letters are there, but they have been rearranged in what is assumed to be meaningless order.)

Looking again at our little piece of ciphertext, we immediately see the predominance of the letter *x*. The letter *x* just doesn't show up that often in any alphabet. No letter does. This may be a clue to the key. It may be that the *x* in that ciphertext isn't intended to be a letter at all. Perhaps it is a *null* character. A null is a character placed within a ciphertext string to either add to confusion or to designate the end of a word or phrase. In either case, in our example, it is a clue to the fact that the string is a cipher, rather than a random set of characters. The *x* wouldn't be nearly so frequent in a random set of characters. Maybe it is a placeholder; maybe it is there to represent spaces between words.

Acting on this assumption, let's look at the message again, this time without all the placeholders:

terces a llet ot woh

It remains in ciphertext, because the message is still not immediately apparent. But now we're beginning to see individual words. We may be on to something.

There are many ways of concocting a transposition cipher. The most common is called a *reverse transposition*. As one would suspect from the name, the letters and/or words are simply presented in reverse order. Reversing the letters in our ciphertext reveals the plaintext message:

how to tell a secret

Congratulations. You've just performed your first feat of *cryptanalysis*.

Cryptanalysis is the science of breaking ciphers and revealing the plaintext message. It has a history as long as that of putting messages into ciphers in the first place.

The ciphertext we revealed was actually a fairly simple exercise. It gets much more complicated as we move on. The first thing that happens is that the words are not kept as distinct units. Following protocols first conceived with the development of the telegraph in the 1830s, letter strings are broken into groups of five. The strings may or may not contain null characters. Using this protocol, our original bit of ciphertext would have read:

xtecr esxax lletx otxwo hxxxx

The next thing that happens is that a more complex matrix of substitution is employed. This is the realm of *geometric ciphers.*

Geometric ciphers rearrange the letters according to a geometric pattern. For example, if our ciphertext message had been placed in a 2-column rectangle, it might look like this:

H	L
O	X
W	A
X	X
T	S
O	E
X	C
T	R
E	E
L	T

The resulting ciphertext would then read:

hloxw axxts oexct reelt

To an experienced cryptologist, it still isn't all that tough. But perhaps we combine the geographic cipher with a reverse cipher, to get:

tleer tcxeo stxxa wxolh

A little tougher. But maybe we start with a substitution cipher, using the Lone Ranger's card. Then go on to the geometric and throw in the reverse. Now we're getting somewhere.

But please don't for a minute think that a rectangle is the only geometric shape available to us as secret-tellers. There are squares—4 columns across, 12 columns across, 100 columns across, and more. And just because we are using a square, we are not confined to placing our letters down the first column and then starting again at the top of the next column. Why not go down and then go up? Why not skip a column and go up (placing null characters in column 2)? And if we can skip 1 column, what is to stop us from skipping 2? Or 6? Or skipping 2 the first time and 5 the next time? And where is it written that we need to go straight up and down? Why not work on a diagonal? A reverse diagonal?

And if we're going to start off with a substitution cipher to begin with, why not run a second substitution on the first? Then we can reverse it, and substitute it yet again before getting to the geometric pattern.

The Bombe

During World War II this computer aided the wizards of Bletchley Park in reading German messages encoded by the Enigma machine. It is now on display at the National Cryptologic Museum at Fort Meade, Maryland. (National Cryptologic Museum)

WORLD WAR II CODE WORDS

Operation Anvil	Allied invasion of the French Riviera
Operation Barbarossa	German invasion of the Soviet Union
Operation Bernhard	German plan to counterfeit British banknotes
Operation Bodyguard	Allied plan of deception and misdirection regarding the date and locale of D-Day
Operation Copperhead	Use of M.E. Clifton-James, as a double of Field Marshall Bernard Montgomery, to confuse Axis intelligence as to the military chief's actual whereabouts
Operation Flash	Plan by a group within the German military to assassinate Hitler. Carried out in July 1944, the attempt was unsuccessful.
Operation Flying Elephant	Japanese plan to firebomb forests in the northwestern United States by launching incendiary balloons. Nearly 10,000 balloons were sent and a few actually made it, but very little damage was caused.
Operation Fortitude	Misdirection by Allied forces in an attempt to have German analysts believe the Normandy landings were a feint with

There is nothing, by the way, to limit us to squares. Trapezoids, circles, triangles, and ovoids are all open to us.

Then, of course, there are random numbers and, well . . . you begin to get the idea. And you begin to see how things can become very complicated very quickly.

To take it one step further: Up to this point, we've done everything by hand.

	the actual invasion coming at Pas-de-Calais
Operation Husky	Allied invasion of Sicily
Operation Iceberg	U.S. invasion of Okinawa
Operation Land of Fire	German plan near the end of the war to relocate looted artwork and gold bullion to Argentina
Operation Long Jump	German plan to assassinate Joseph Stalin, Winston Churchill, and Franklin Roosevelt during the Tehran Conference in late November 1943
Operation Meeting House	Allied firebombing of Tokyo in March 1945
Operation Overlord	Allied invasion of continental Europe in June 1944; the code word was reportedly coined by Churchill
Operation Paperclip	Plan to capture German rocket scientists, and then transport them to the United States
Operation Pastorius	German plan to land spies and saboteurs in the United States; named after Franz Pastorius, who in 1683 became the first German immigrant to the New World
Operation Sea Lion	German plan for the invasion of England
Operation Torch	Allied invasion of North Africa
Operation Z	Japanese attack on Pearl Harbor

Think what a computer could do with all this if the right software were written.

Computers began to get into the act during World War II. They would pound through thousands upon thousands of letter combinations and substitutions in the ciphertext until the plaintext became clear. Since that time, of course, there have been advances in computer technology.

CODES

Cryptographers will tell you that a *code* is a fairly simple method of substituting one thing for another. Usually it is done with words, but it may be accomplished with a string of numbers or graphic symbols. Generally speaking, one new symbol (be it a word, number string, or picture) is substituted for another, plaintext word or a larger thing. It becomes a shorthand way of referring to the original.

During World War II an elaborate system of code words was used to designate military operations, the idea being that even if a code word was overheard or learned, the secret operation that lay behind it may not be penetrated.

Codes need not be secret. The bar codes commonly used during a supermarket checkout are a good example, since there is nothing secret about them. There are two parts to the code: the numbers and the machine-readable graphics.

Each product contains a unique identifying number. This number will designate the manufacturer, the nature of the product, and other information specific to that individual product (when it was ordered from the manufacturer, when it came into the store, etc.). The identifying number is translated into a graphic representation, a series of vertical lines that allow the product to be quickly scanned by the register's system. By design, no two sets of vertical lines are alike. This allows the

SOS

The international Morse code distress call ("S-O-S") does not stand for "save our ship." It doesn't actually stand for anything.

The code for letters S (three dots) and O (three dashes) are merely the easiest to learn and quickest to send. And generally speaking, a little alacrity and a little less obfuscation are positive elements in an urgent situation.

computer to properly price the item at the checkout, to keep track of inventory left on the shelves, and, by the way, to capture a number of other data points (such as the time and date of the transaction, the other products purchased at the same time and during the same transaction, and, if a credit card, debit card, or store discount card is used, the name and address of the person making the purchase). None of this information is necessarily secret. It is the combination of the bar code and computer system that allows the store to gather quickly and easily all the information it may need to record the transaction. The bar code then becomes a shorthand for the product itself.

In a similar way, Morse code is not secret. Originally developed in the 1830s by Samuel Morse, it is a way of converting a plaintext message into electronic impulses. These impulses, a series of short and long bursts (often called dots and dashes, respectively), can be read by a skilled operator and converted back to the plaintext message. It was used extensively by telegraph operators during the middle and late nineteenth century. By the 1890s, it had become the accepted international code for early radio communications.

But many codes are secret. Serious development of the concept can be traced to the European diplomatic corps. Deep within the archives of the Vatican are examples of coded communications between the various city-states surrounding the Mediterranean dating to the 1300s. They are elaborate systems designed to guard against correct interpretation of messages intercepted by rivals.

Extensive vocabularies were constructed. To keep track of it all, special dictionaries were compiled. They were originally written on parchment; as the number of pages grew, they were collated and placed between covers for protection against the casual (and, perhaps, not so casual) observer. These were the first codebooks.

Problems began to arise almost immediately with this system. The first problem was that if you had one dictionary, you really needed at least two: one for the writer and one for the reader. Having two copies of the codebook doubled the chances that it would be lost or stolen. Having 12 copies or 50 copies increased those chances all the more. If one is missing, you must assume that it has been stolen and that the entire system is compromised. Then you have to start all over again.

The next problem was being caught with a codebook in your possession. There was no easy way to explain this away to the authorities, and spies became all the more vulnerable.

Finally, as the codes became larger and more extensive, they became cumbersome. There are instances when you just don't have a lot of time to sit down to encode or decode a message. There could be someone pounding on the door or the train could be leaving in 10 minutes or perhaps the enemy had just boarded your ship. There are times when you just have things to do other than figure out what 3456.34.2954 means, particularly when the codebook contains everything from "the enemy marches tonight" to "reception at the baron's palace went well."

The quickest solution to the problem was to decentralize the codes. In other words, to have one code for diplomats, another for the army, still another for the navy. Perhaps yet another for communications between a unit in the field and the headquarters. Still, priority had to be given to keeping the codebooks secure.

One way of doing this was to hide the book in plain sight. Rather than a specialized book, cryptographers began to construct codes using commonplace books—a dictionary, for example.

Suppose you, as the president of a country, wanted to send a coded message to your general in the field. You could use an established codebook. Or you could see to it that your general had exactly the same edition of the dictionary that sat on your desk. This way, you could send something along the lines of

$$124.12 \qquad 135.86 \qquad 136.4 \qquad 111.9$$

If your general had the same dictionary, he could turn to page 124 and count down to word number 12 and see the word *how*; then to page 135, word number 86 and see *is*; then to page 136, word number 4, and see *it*; and page 111, word number 9, and see *going*. The general would get the message and reply in kind.

This is not a hypothetical situation. It is exactly what Jefferson Davis, president of the Confederate States of America, writing in his office in Richmond, Virginia, did with General Albert Sydney Johnson, who was fighting Union armies in Corinth, Mississippi. And it worked.

With the coming of telegraphy, the need for codes and ciphers increased exponentially. This was the case not only for the military and diplomatic corps but also for commerce. In part this was to keep things secret (stock transactions, fluctuations in prices, and the like) but also to cut costs.

Sending a telegram could be an expensive proposition, since the sender was charged by the word group. (Remember the five-digit letter string?) So if a five-digit code could be successfully implemented, costs could be reduced substantially. Sending 59382 was much less expensive than sending "Ship the goods by tomorrow's train." It became all the more important when the transatlantic cable was laid in 1866.

But there was always the chance that 59382 did not mean "Ship the goods by tomorrow's train." It just might mean something else entirely. And that something was supposed to remain secret. And again, we're back to the problem of security. At least two people had to know what 59382 meant, and that brings us full circle to codebooks and all those pesky problems.

One ingenious way of confounding those who attempted to penetrate the numerical codes was to double-encrypt the message. In other words, to first create the ciphertext, then add a second level of encryption to that. This could be done very simply by the application of an *additive*. An additive is a standard number that is simply added to the code.

For example, let us assume that our additive is *12345*. So

$$
\begin{array}{ll}
59382 & \text{(code)} \\
+\underline{12345} & \text{(additive)} \\
71727 & \text{(encrypted code)}
\end{array}
$$

The receiver of the telegram simply subtracts 12345 from 71730 to get the code. Since the additive is standard for the entire telegram, the encryption is easily translated into the complete coded message. Without the key (that is, without knowing what the additive is), anyone who intercepted the telegram would have no way of getting back to the original message without extensive trial and error. Thus, even if the codebooks had been compromised, the added level of encryption would render an intercepted telegram meaningless. For still added security, the additive would be changed periodically. And then begin the variations: one additive for the army, another for the navy, another for the diplomats.

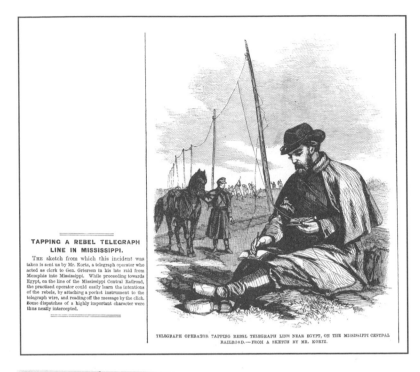

TAPPING A REBEL TELEGRAPH LINE IN MISSISSIPPI.

THE sketch from which this incident was taken is sent us by Mr. Kortz, a telegraph operator who acted as clerk to Gen. Grierson in his late raid from Memphis into Mississippi. While proceeding towards Egypt, on the line of the Mississippi Central Railroad, the practised operator could easily learn the intentions of the rebels, by attaching a pocket instrument to the telegraph wire, and reading off the message by the click. Some dispatches of a highly important character were thus neatly intercepted.

TELEGRAPH OPERATOR TAPPING REBEL TELEGRAPH LINE NEAR EGYPT, ON THE MISSISSIPPI CENTRAL RAILROAD.—FROM A SKETCH BY MR. KORTZ.

Tapping the Lines

Generals on both sides of the conflict found it profitable to keep skilled telegraph operators in their commands during the Civil War. Not only could a skilled operator send messages from the field but he could also tap the enemy's lines and intercept messages. Not quite so profitable, however, were the activities of newspaper correspondents who traveled with the commands and would share secrets, like this one, for all to see. *From Frank Leslie's Illustrated Newspaper,* March 15, 1865. (Courtesy of the Virginia Room of the Arlington County Public Library)

This was important, since telegraph lines were fairly easy to tap by a skilled operator. Both sides in the American Civil War took advantage of the breaches in security.

The world has changed since the introduction of the telegraph, of course. Communications have become much more sophisticated, as have the methods of intercepting them. Any message, sent via any form of transit (telegraph, word of mouth, dead drop, carrier pigeon, microdot, computer e-mail, cell phone . . . you name it) is subject to interception. All that protects the secrecy of the message is the level of encryption of the message.

Codes and ciphers must be changed with regularity. The more samples of your code in the other side's hands, the better are the chances that they will penetrate its mysteries. Code words and patterns will repeat themselves, giving clues as to hidden meanings. (Remember the x in our original bit of ciphertext?) It doesn't take a skilled cryptologist long to follow the clues.

The first defense against this is keeping the messages from being intercepted in the first place.

STEGANOGRAPHY

The single best way of keeping a secret is by not telling it to anyone. If I first assume that I can trust myself completely, I must next assume that I cannot trust you quite as completely. It then follows that I cannot trust the person you're going to talk to as much as I trust you. Or the person she talks to. Carry this out several places and you begin to visualize a security officer's worst-case scenario.

Still, keeping a secret to yourself isn't nearly as productive (or, at times, as much fun) as sharing it with someone. It is in the sharing, however, that danger of exposure first appears.

Ciphers and codes, complex as they may be, can be broken. The sad fact is that there is always someone out there who is just a little smarter than you are. And no matter your level of commitment to keeping your communications secure, there is someone lurking in the bushes with at least the same level of commitment to making your communications wholly transparent.

So perhaps the second best way of keeping a secret is not letting the guy in the bushes know that the secret exists in the first place. Even the fact that you've got a secret is a secret.

It is time to think about secret writing and some methods of misdirection.

In 1967 historian David Kahn coined the term *steganography* to cover this endeavor. It means, quite literally, "hidden or covered writing." It is the art and the science of concealing the fact that a message even exists.

This is spy stuff: briefcases with hidden compartments, hollow boot heels, and hidden pockets inside the sleeves of a sport coat. Dead drops. Invisible inks and microdots. The loose brick in the wall and the tube of toothpaste that neither contains toothpaste nor is even a tube.

It is nothing new. The ancient Chinese, in the days before the Great Kahn, would write their secrets on small bits of extremely thin rice paper, roll the paper into a tiny ball, dip it in wax, and hide it, like a bit of lint, on the messenger. If the messenger were then stopped along the way for any reason, the "lint" would be passed over during a search.

But as we have seen, as civilization and technology advance, so do the ways in which we tell secrets. So it is with the ways we hide them.

Hiding in plain sight has always been the best method. Things would be much easier for our ancient Chinese messenger if the only people who knew he was a messenger were those who sent him on his mission and met him on its completion. If anyone else knew what he was up to, things might get complicated.

Suspicions are aroused when something begins to draw attention to itself. Thus, a codebook in one's suitcase is a dead giveaway; a common dictionary is not (unless it is the only book being carried). Someone looking nervous and sweating on a winter's day is going to draw far more attention to themselves than if they were simply sitting in a coffee shop with the day's newspaper.

By definition, a message written in invisible ink cannot be seen by the naked eye without some sort of treatment. However, that same message might draw attention to its presence if it is written on a blank piece of paper that has been carefully wrapped and placed inside a sealed envelope. Much better to write the message between the lines of a book. Better still if the book is just one of several that you just happen to be carrying in a backpack.

Likewise, a microdot the size of a period on this page, traveling alone on a blank

HOW TO WRITE A SECRET MESSAGE

1. Go to the supermarket.
2. Buy a lemon.
3. Take it home and squeeze the juice out.
4. Start writing with the juice and a paintbrush.

Actually, nearly any citrus juice will do. Onion juice works too. Once written, the "ink" disappears from plain view. It will be made visible again by holding the treated paper over a lightbulb.

Writing a secret message is one thing. Keeping your message hidden is another matter altogether. That takes some practice and perhaps a little tradecraft.

The first thing that you want to make sure of is that no one (other than the recipient) knows that there is a message there.

The idea is to hide the message in plain sight. In other words, your message should be written on something that everyone can see but that no one will really look at. The objective here is normalcy. When you are stopped, everything should appear matter of course, so investigations will go no further.

Writing over the pages of a book works nicely, if it is not extraordinary that you're carrying a book around. We want no one to look twice at your treated book, so the book in question should be one of several that you're carrying; all the books should be more or less in the same state of repair. It would be nice if there were a reason for you to be carrying books, so a

sheet of paper, is going to stick out like a sore thumb. On the other hand, that same microdot, perhaps placed under a stamp on an envelope that has been dropped into a corner mailbox, has a much better chance of getting through the mail without detection.

Tradecraft is that set of skills intelligence officers employ when carrying out clandestine operations. The term encompasses a wide and varied group of tech-

cover should be concocted (you're a student, for example). The books should relate in some way to your cover.

Don't crack the spine to the page where you've written the message. If you do, get another book. When you are stopped and searched, you don't want the book to automatically open to the page you've treated. Once you've written the message, crack the spine many times, always at random (but not on the page you've treated), so no one page will stick out. While you're at it, read the book. If you're carrying around a book with a cracked spine, you want to be able to answer questions about it if someone should ask (otherwise, it would be suspicious that you're carrying a well-read book that you know nothing about).

As long as we're talking about normalcy, keep in mind that few books smell like lemons. So when you do your writing, be sparing of the juice and try not to spill any on the pages.

Next: don't use a pen, pencil, or any instrument that may leave an impression on the page. It's a dead giveaway that there's something there. A paintbrush works best for laying down the message. It won't leave an impression on the page, and it is easy to dip into your ink.

Pick the right kind of paper too. The glossy paper used in a magazine is not at all suitable. When your ink dries, the coded area will look distinctly different from the surrounding area. It is best to pick a porous or fibrous paper, something along the lines of a newspaper. You want your ink to soak in a little bit without leaving any sort of mark when you're done.

niques, all designed to keep things hidden. The successful intelligence officer does not want things to look "normal." The successful intelligence officer is one who has succeeded in not having anyone take a look, and thereby passing judgments, in the first place.

Please don't misunderstand: We are *not* talking about James Bond here. Everyone, including the bad guys, knew who James Bond was, knew that he was referred to as

007, and had a pretty good idea of what he was up to. The only real secret associated with James Bond was that he got away with as much as he did.

And Maxwell Smart, with his shoe phone and *86* emblazoned on his bathrobe, is no role model either. The star of the 1960s situation comedy *Get Smart*, Agent 86, wouldn't have made it past the opening credits if he were operating in the real world. (To begin with, he never would have found a place to park on the street outside his office in Washington, D.C.)

Tradecraft is serious business. If you're to be a successful officer, you must be not only above suspicion but also above suspicion of suspicion. To do that, you must not merely blend into your surroundings. You must be nearly as invisible as your ink.

Keeping a normal routine, for example, can be a giveaway. There's very little that is "normal" about everyday life. While some people may go directly to the office each morning by the most efficient route, eat their lunches at their desks, and go right home from work, not many do. There are always side trips (to the dry cleaners or the market or the bookstore). These must be taken into account.

There are skills to master for surveillance and countersurveillance. There are cover stories to construct and plausible reasons to be doing something or being somewhere that you really shouldn't be doing or being.

There is the entire realm of disguise—when to use it, when to avoid it. How much is too much? Is the combination of a floppy hat and sunglasses enough? Would walking with a limp be appropriate? And above all, you have to remember to keep it up. Wearing the sling on your right arm on Monday and on your left arm on Wednesday isn't going to fly.

Perhaps most important, you've got to keep it simple. Or at least make it appear simple. If it is too complicated, too convoluted, it will be difficult to maintain or remember in a critical situation. Worse, if it is too complicated, it may be too noticeable. Consistency is the imperative, because sometimes you may have to be just a little inconsistent.

Once tradecraft has been mastered, secret writing awaits.

There are many kinds of invisible inks, for example. Some are made from citrus juice or onion juice. They do have the benefit of simplicity. At the same time, they have the very real disadvantage of being well known. During World War II, a reverse

ink was used. Flyers carried maps printed, with special ink, on silk handkerchiefs. In case of capture, they were to soak the silk in urine to cause the ink to disappear.

During the American Revolution, Sir James Jay, brother of John Jay, first chief justice of the U.S. Supreme Court, concocted an ink that required one chemical for the writing and treatment of the document on the other end with another chemical for the reading. The "sympathetic stain," as it was called, would be applied to a plain white piece of paper and sent on its way. The receiver would then brush a corresponding compound on the paper when it reached its destination. The formula Jay concocted, by the way, has never been replicated. Complicated stuff, but General Washington (America's first spymaster) seemed to like it and gave detailed instructions for its use. (The good general, it should be noted, chose to write those instructions in plaintext.)

But the use of invisible inks is just one form of secret writing. In addition to codes and ciphers, what appears to be a normal letter to the casual observer—or even to an overworked censor—can hide messages. The spaces between words, the shape of the letters, the upward or downward slash of a crossed *t*, the shape of the upper part of the letter *d*, for example, or the lower part of the letter *j*, the position of the dot on top of an *i*—all can (and have been used to) transmit messages.

There are also mechanical devices, such as the *grille* first employed by Italian physician Girolamo Cardano in the sixteenth century. It was an ingenious device.

Once the message was composed, it was hidden within a larger plaintext document. A stiff piece of paper was placed over the document, and holes were cut over the important words. The two were then sent, via separate routes, to the receiver. At the far end, the grille would be matched to the document and the secret writing would be revealed, since only the words of the secret writing would be visible. The downside of this method was the need to compose around the words required for the message. The language often became awkward and intercepted documents would violate the first rule: They were noticed.

A variation of this technique is to use a series of prearranged words or syllables. Compose a poem and have your recipient read only the first letter of each line:

Mellow flows the river of
Eaton, beyond the shadow of the

Elm, to the land where my love
Tarries in moonlight gardens.
My soul rises at the sound of her
Ever light step.
'Twixt the day and the night,
Only a feverish glance,
Nay, a trembling look,
In wonder's past can possibly
Grant this dream to flower.
Harken to the song of the river . . .
'Twill quench thy thirst!

The poem doesn't even have to be good (obviously); it just has to get by the censors. But the first letter of each line, if read straight down, comprises the message.

In a similar way, using only every third word in a document, or only the capitalized words or perhaps those with a dot of invisible ink above it, can hide a greater meaning in an innocent-looking document. The trick is to make it sound natural; forced or stilted language is bound to catch the censor's eye.

Prior to America's entry to World War I, Germany was concerned that the United States would join the war on the side of the Western Allies. A number of German spy rings worked in the United States. As a cover, one such group acted as legitimate journalists covering developments in the United States. At first glance it made sense, since journalists are always writing things and foreign journalists are always sending stories back to their newspapers.

The problem they faced with that era's technology was the best way of sending a story: via the commercial telegraph networks. If messages were to be contained, they must be in secret writing.

American censors picked up on this one:

President's embargo ruling should have immediate notice. Grave situation affecting international law. Statement foreshadows ruin of many neutrals. Yellow journals unifying national excitement immensely.

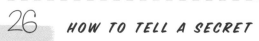

The language didn't seem quite right, and censors picked it up and began to take a second look. Several days later, a second cable crossed their desks. Apparently it was sent to verify the first:

Apparently neutral's protest is thoroughly discounted and ignored. Isman hard hit. Blockade issue affects pretext for Embargo on byproducts, ejecting suets and vegetable oils.

This one, too, deserved a second look.

The censors found that by pulling the first letter of each word in the first message, and the second letter of each word in the second message, the following appeared in plaintext:

Pershing sails from NY June 1.

It was a good try, but Pershing had actually sailed earlier, so no damage was done to the Allied war efforts. The sender never was identified.

Strictly speaking, secret writing doesn't have to be written. It can cross transmission media, although here we begin to bump into the realms of codes and ciphers. The point is to get the message past the censor and the casual observer.

Talking to "the guy" about "the thing" is an example that springs to mind. And the use of jargon in nontraditional ways may work too. Specifying "two cases of olives" within an otherwise innocent order could easily mean two divisions of infantry.

Even if your message is invisible to the guy lurking in the bushes, you still will want to hide the fact that it is being sent along its way. For accomplishing this, dead drops have been the tool of choice for centuries.

The use of a dead drop eliminates the possibility that the two parties involved in the transmission (the sender and the receiver) will ever meet. The way it works is that a hidden location in a public space becomes the repository for the message. Perhaps it's a hole in the tree trunk of that old elm in the park. Maybe the space between cinder blocks in a parking garage downtown. Maybe under a rock in the stream (perhaps under a bridge?) that runs along the bike path in the woods. If there is a plausible reason for both parties to occasionally visit the spot, it could work.

ELECTRONIC DEAD DROP

Tradecraft in general, and dead drops in particular, evolve with technology.

Published reports show that the September 11, 2001, terrorist attack on the World Trade Center and Pentagon (9/11) used a high-tech, very secure, and essentially free method of communication prior to their attacks. Knowing that no encryption technology is entirely foolproof, they chose to send messages without actually transmitting them.

The reasoning was good: If messages were not actually transmitted—that is, if they did not go out over the Internet or cell phones or land lines or even through the postal system—there was no danger of their being intercepted. Without interception, of course, the messages would never be read regardless of ciphers or codes.

So a Hotmail account was established. Hotmail is a free service that allows the user to send e-mail over the Internet. The user logs on to the system server over the Internet to access his account. He writes his e-mail, designates the intended receiver's e-mail address, clicks on a button . . . and off it goes.

However, if the mail is not actually sent, the message goes nowhere. It just sits in the user's outbox or drafts folder. And it will continue to sit there, on the service's computer, until the account owner either sends it or deletes it.

Since it doesn't actually go anywhere, it cannot be intercepted.

The terrorists used the Hotmail account as a dead drop. One would log on to the account and compose a message, saving it as a draft (that is, a message in the works that could be retrieved, perhaps edited, and sent at a later time). Later in the day, another terrorist working from another location would log on to the same account and read the "draft" message, deleting it when he was done.

On Monday, the sender visits the spot and deposits the message. He then sends a signal, one innocent to the observer, that the message is in place. The signal may be the set of his window blinds, a stray chalk mark on a park bench, or even the fact that he chooses to wear the same tie two days in a row. Once the signal is seen, the receiver visits the dead drop, in what may appear to be an innocent visit to a public locale, and retrieves the message.

A message need not be secret to be clandestine. During World War II, the British Broadcasting Company (the BBC) broadcast a series of phrases to occupied Europe. Seemingly meaningless—isolated lyrics of songs, lines of poetry, random phrases—they would go out every night. Part of the misdirection was in their random sequence and the fact that they went every night.

But the phrases weren't random. This was a verbal form of steganography. The message was there, but it was hidden. Resistance cells would listen to the broadcasts on forbidden radios in hidden meeting places. Often they didn't know what the messages meant or for whom they were intended. Sometimes there would be only one significant phrase in a 15-minute broadcast. Often there were no phrases of interest to anyone in the "personal messages" broadcast each night. But every once in a long while a phrase would send chills down the listeners' collective spines, for the messages were directed to that cell on that night giving them a specific set of instructions.

The German Abwehr, the military intelligence group that successfully discovered the penetration of the embassy in Lisbon, discovered the jargon-code that would be employed to alert French Resistance forces of the impending invasion. It was to be in two parts. The first would signal that the invasion was imminent. It was to come in the form of the first half of the first stanza of "Chanson d'Automne," a poem by Paul Verlaine, broadcast on either the first or the fifteenth day of the month. The second part was a call to action, for it foretold the coming of Allied forces. When the second half of the stanza was broadcast, the Resistance (and the Abwehr) would know that the invasion would take place within 48 hours.

On the night of June 5, 1944, at 9:15 PM, to be exact, they heard:

wound my heart with a monotonous languor

A CODE WORD FOR VICTORY

The international Morse code designation for the letter *V* became shorthand for the word *victory* during World War II.

Three short pulses followed by a long pulse (three dots and a dash) came to stand for Allied victory over the Axis forces in Europe.

The symbol was used on patriotic materials (lapel pins, mo- rale posters, etc.). It would be flashed by the landing lights of Allied aircraft.

Victory from the World War II home front. This lapel pin was worn on the American home front, with pride and hope, during the war years. The three dots and a dash are shorthand for the Morse code designation for the letter *V*. They also stood for the opening notes of Beethoven's Fifth Symphony. *(Kismet Images)*

It was the second half of the stanza, and it meant the invasion was on. The Abwehr monitored the broadcast and knew what it meant. They sounded the alarm.

One of the great unsolved mysteries of World War II was why the German army was taken by surprise by the D-Day invasion. They knew what was coming; they knew what to listen for; they heard what they were listening for. But for reasons that have never been fully explained, they chose to ignore the broadcast message.

The Ancients

An American Wayside Inn, 1858

THE TAVERN KEEPER HAD A PROBLEM. IT WAS DIFFICULT ENOUGH attempting to keep a copper or two ahead of the mortgage on the place. Rough-hewn were the beams on the ceilings and the patrons alike. Mud was everywhere. Mud from the fields and mud from the roads. Mud on the boots and on the jackets and on the people who would stop to pass the time over a companion pint of the best brew.

When the men would drink, they would smoke and chew the essence of Virginia's first cash crop, tobacco. Since its introduction by the Indians some generations before, the men visiting taverns throughout the colonies, and later the states, had partaken of the weed in its variety of forms, with filler for ornate or crudely constructed pipes, big ugly cigars, and the chaw in the cheek being the most popular choices. Snuff was for dandies, who didn't often visit these ruder haunts.

The problem wasn't the tobacco smoke. The smell and haze derived from the burning of organic material was a fact of everyday life. Fire was the principal means of both cooking and heat, after all. And the absence of an open hearth, or one of Dr. Franklin's potbelllied stoves, would have been cause for comment. A little smoke, more or less, wouldn't have made much of a difference in the taproom.

The problem was with the leavings. Burned tobacco produces ashes. Chewed tobacco produces a rather unpleasant type and volume of expectorate. Cigars that have completed their mission leave stubs. All of this had to go somewhere.

Unfortunately for our tavern keeper, this somewhere was often on his tables or floor. It was chore enough to keep the mud away; not much could be done about that. But the tobacco leavings! At the end of any given day it was just plain nasty in there. And no one wanted to step (or sit) in someone else's leavings.

It was a problem not just for tavern keepers. In 1842, Charles Dickens toured the United States on the lecture circuit. His description of the halls of Congress, rendered perhaps as only Dickens could, described the situation under the yet-to-be-completed Capitol dome:

> Both houses are handsomely carpeted, but the state to which these carpets are reduced by the universal disregard of the spittoon with which every honorable member is accommodated, and the extraordinary improvements on the pattern which are squirted and dabbled upon it in every direction, do not admit of being described. I will merely observe that I strongly recommend all strangers not to look at the floor; and if they happen to drop anything . . . not to pick it up with an ungloved hand on any account.

Enter Messrs. Currier and Ives with a solution in the form of a *rebus*.

Mid-nineteenth-century America, like much of the world, was a largely illiterate place. Schooling for the young was not compulsory. It was the norm to spend only a year or two in the classroom; for most of the population, the skills acquired with letters and numbers were rudimentary at best. For much of the population, reading in the home was confined to the Bible, and even then much of the effort was placed on the ornate images engraved on those pages.

The combination of text and images to provide a unified message was neither new nor unique to America, of course. Some of the earliest forms of writing conveyed messages through the use of pictures, rather than letters. But as alphabets became established, character sets were used to represent a word; using a picture to represent an object became an archaic means of expression. As literacy (the ability to translate letters into words) grew, the need to depict the picture of an object

to represent the actual object, diminished. Combining letters and pictures into a single document (called a rebus) to convey a message became an entertainment. It was fun to perform the mental gymnastics required to jump between reading words and interpreting pictures to derive a single, unified message.

By 1834 Currier & Ives was a New York City–based firm billed as "Publishers of Cheap and Popular Pictures." Some chroniclers put their output in excess of 7,000 distinct lithographic prints, most of which were priced between 5 and 25 cents— none for more than $3.

Artists and publishers they were. And astute businessmen, too. They saw a need and they set out to fill it. With our tavern keeper and others of his ilk in mind, they created a lithographic print directed toward those who would indulge in the misuse of tobacco. Without wishing to preach, they created an admonishment to be posted on taverns' walls in the form of a rebus.

THE REBUS

The earliest examples of the rebus may be found in the Nile River valley in Egypt. The ancient Egyptians, credited with some of the earliest ciphertext messages, have also been credited with the development of the rebus as a means of communication. That use, though, was not intended to obscure the message. Hieroglyphics, an alphabet of picture-symbols, was intended to represent specific sounds and ideas native to Egyptian culture. The use of additional symbols was intended to add clarity to the message.

Modern use of the rebus has been traced to the Picardy region of France. At the beginning of the seventeenth century, during carnival, a group of students and clerks would make disparaging remarks about events and people of the times. But to retain a bit of anonymity, they would do so in a circumspect

Roosevelt Rebus

This political campaign button was worn during the presidential election of 1904 by a supporter of Theodore "Teddy" Roosevelt. (Hake's Americana)

way. They would make a game of it by replacing words with pictures that would sound like the words. They would then distribute their satires as *de rebus quae gerunter,* a Latin phrase translating to "of things which are going on."

Keep in mind that the world was largely an illiterate place until the latter half of the 1800s. Telling a story through symbols and pictures was commonplace, almost necessary, when the audience couldn't read. Pictures helped to clarify the message.

One of the more famous American rebuses was created and distributed by Ben Franklin (a pretty crafty businessman in his own right). His, entitled "The Art of Making Money Plenty," went through a number of printings (including one by the firm of Currier & Ives).

As literacy rates grew, the rebus evolved from a teaching tool to an entertainment. Although not true steganography, since the message contained isn't intended to be secret, a good rebus still sought to convey a message without that

Franklin's Rebus

When rendered in plaintext, the rebus reads: "The Art of Making Money Plenty in every Man's Pocket by Doctor Franklin. At this time when the major complaint is that money is so scarce it must be an act of kindness to instruct the moneyless how they can reinforce their pockets. I will acquaint you with the true secret of money catching, the certain way to fill empty purses and how to keep them always full. Two simple rules well observed will do the business. First, let honesty and labor be thy constant companions. Second, spend one penny every day less than thy clear gains. Then shall thy pockets soon begin to thrive, thy creditors will never insult thee, nor want oppress, nor hunger bite, nor nakedness freeze thee; the whole hemisphere will shine brighter, and pleasure spring up in every corner of thy heart. Now therefore embrace these rules and be Happy."

message being immediately discernible. The message was not in plaintext; it was hidden in plain sight. Viewed in this light, a rebus is a form of secret writing. So to be precise, a rebus could be a form of steganography, but perhaps steganography that winks at the reader. It was fun to decipher the meaning. The more obscure the reference included in the rebus, the more fun was to be had in the solving.

The partnership of Nathaniel Currier and James Merritt Ives, purveyors of colored engravings for the people, as one of their mastheads proclaimed, provided a solution in the form of the rebus reprinted above. It was specifically designed for public places such as taverns and bars. Not only was it fun to work through the meanings hidden in the pictures but also the message would be all the more memorable because the process of uncovering the overall hidden meaning took some discussion and wit.

The rebus continues to flourish. Technically, the modern rebus is a kind of *proto-writing*, placing it neatly between the worlds of mass communication and steganography. A rebus uses *pictograms,* graphic representations as a means of conveying sounds, words, or ideas. Many signs found on restroom doors are pictograms, with stick figures differentiating the doors through which men may pass from those through which women may pass.

PICTOGRAMS

The earliest form of written communication was the pictogram.

The artwork painted or scratched on the walls of prehistoric caves in southern Europe attempt to tell a story through the use of pictures. Archeologists date some of these cave paintings to 18,000 BCE. They most certainly predate a written language, but the general idea is there: to represent a sound or a thing with a graphic image.

Perhaps the best-known example of ancient writing can be found in the hieroglyphics developed by Egyptian scribes. This is a highly organized system, using nearly 700 individual picture-symbols to represent the sounds and ideas of Egyptian culture and language. The system is actually a bridge, of sorts, between pre-

PROTOWRITING

Protowriting is a technical term that encompasses all forms of graphic communication employed prior to the development of a formal script or alphabet. All protowriting falls into one of two distinct categories: the ideogram (ideograph) and the logogram (logogriph).

Generally speaking, *ideograms* use a symbol or a picture to depict a specific thing or an idea. The term comes from the Greek *idea*, meaning, well, "idea," and *gramma*, meaning drawn. Pictograms are a type of ideogram. Although the thing being represented by the ideogram may have a name or a word associated with it, the image represents the thing rather than the word.

The *logogram*, on the other hand,

Ideogram

historic pictograms and modern alphabets, since some of the symbols represent objects, while others represent the sounds of the verbal language.

Actually, it was in the recognition that the system was, in fact, a bridge that allowed for its eventual translation. That one "bridge" concept was the key that allowed the secret of the hieroglyphic system to be breached. Up to that point, hieroglyphic inscriptions were ciphertext and could not be read. Once the key was applied, the message could be rendered in plaintext.

The existence of these strange inscriptions throughout the Nile River valley was well known, of course. Etched in stone or painted on walls, they decorated pillar, pyramid, and tomb and would regularly turn up in archeological digs (authorized and not) throughout the region. But the meanings behind the inscriptions had been lost. And there was no way to go back and ask a scribe what everything meant.

uses a graphic to represent a sound or a word. This term is also from the Greek: *logos*, meaning "word," and again, *gramma*, meaning "drawn." It is from logograms that alphabets were developed.

The distinction between the two is important to the understanding of the development of formalized alphabets.

The earliest system of formalized writing, of what we have come to think of as an alphabet, came from Mesopotamia in the form of *cuneiform*. The earliest examples date from 3300 BCE. The samples that survive show it to be a series of uniform, stylized slashes that were cut into clay tablets. Scholars believe that it evolved from earlier pictographs, when scribes simplified the elaborate graphic

Logogram

pictures that had been employed up to that time. Somebody realized that it was a lot easier to write *cow* (or its Mesopotamian equivalent) than to draw a picture of one. It became a kind of shorthand, and it caught on.

American Pictoglyph

Prehistoric symbols, circa 1200 to 1300 CE painted on a rock wall at Fountain Bluff in Jackson County, Illinois (Photri/Microstock)

THE ROSETTA STONE AND HIEROGLYPHICS

Until, that is, Napoleon figured out a way of doing it.

It was in the late spring of 1798. The rulers of postrevolutionary France (the French Revolution, followed by the Reign of Terror, had removed the traditional French monarchy and replaced it with a rudimentary democracy a few years earlier) were growing just a bit concerned about their hotheaded and very ambitious young general. The man was very good on a battlefield. He commanded both troops and luck and overcame astounding odds, multinational armies, and entire countries with remarkable, almost frightening, ease. The fear, not ungrounded, as it would turn out, was that he would next turn his ambitions back toward the seat of power in Paris. So the French Directory, the council of five directors then ruling the country, sent Napoleon to Egypt in May 1798.

Sailing with a force of nearly 40,000 men, including some 300 scientists, Napo-

The Rosetta Stone

Now on display in the British Museum in London, was the key to turning ancient Egyptian hieroglyphics from ciphertext to plaintext. (Kismet Images)

leon landed in Alexandria on July 1. The French forces under Napoleon quickly overcame the Mameluke rulers of the country (he lost 18 men to more than 1,600 defenders). Napoleon then set out to conquer the mysteries of the pharaohs.

During a series of expeditions down the Nile River valley, his scientists catalogued the ruins they found. Detailed drawings were made of the hieroglyphic inscriptions. Tombs were opened. Obelisks and mummies and sections of temple walls were packed and shipped back to Europe. Still, the inscriptions remained in ciphertext, until one group unearthed what came to be known as the Rosetta stone. It was a solid slab of black basalt weighing nearly three quarters of a ton.

One side, polished smooth, carried inscriptions in two languages (Egyptian and Greek) and three scripts (hieroglyphics at the top, a more recent Egyptian script in the middle, and Greek at the bottom).

The bottom two scripts were well known. Scholars were able to compare the inscription at the bottom of the stone, in Greek, to the inscription in the middle (it was in Middle Demotic, to be precise, used between roughly 400 to 30 BCE) and see that they contained the same message. From there, it wasn't a huge leap of logic to assume that the hieroglyphics contained the identical message. Still, there were pieces that didn't quite fit.

The story begins to get long and complicated. Representations of the Rosetta stone were distributed among scholars throughout Europe, and the findings each made were shared among colleagues. Slowly the ciphertext became plaintext.

But it wasn't until nearly 20 years later that Jean-François Champollion finally made the breakthrough discovery. Work until that point had proceeded under the assumption that the hieroglyphic inscriptions had been purely pictoglyphs—that is, it was believed that each picture represented an entire word. Through a detailed analysis, Champollion discovered that the hieroglyphic symbols outnumbered the Greek characters by nearly 3 to 1. Clearly this was not a case of one symbol equaling one word.

The stone carried three versions of a royal decree commemorating the first anniversary of the coronation of Egyptian Pharaoh Ptolemy V. Ptolemy is a Greek name (the line was actually descended from Alexander the Great). Champollion postulated that the inscriptions contained within rectangular boxes (called cartouches) represented sounds rather than words. Working with this hypothesis, he was able to locate the cartouche representing Ptolemy and break the symbols down to the sounds they represented.

It was the understanding of the nature of hieroglyphics—that is, that they were a bridge between pictograms (entire words) and ideograms (individual sounds)—that was the key required to translate the Rosetta stone's ciphertext (the hieroglyphics) to plaintext.

During the years-long process of translating hieroglyphic inscriptions to contemporary languages, some interesting cryptanalysis-related discoveries were made. The first was the earliest known use of a rebus. It came in the name of King Narmer.

This king was the first to rule a unified ancient Egypt, circa 3150 BCE. His name is depicted as a chisel (representing the *mr* sound) and a catfish (representing the *n'r* sound). It is a little difficult to tell from existing records, but he might have actually been called "King Catfish."

As interesting as King Catfish may have been, there is, to the cryptanalytic mind, an even more interesting tidbit to be gleaned from the ancient Egyptians. Their tombs contain the earliest known examples of enciphered text.

The inscriptions one met when passing a tomb were prayers, of sorts, for the person inside. Just as a headstone in a Colonial New England burial ground may implore, "Stranger, stop and stay awhile . . . ," the inscriptions on Egyptian tombs tell the life story of the deceased, with a final request for prayers. Scholars believe that after a period, the inscriptions tended to be ignored by passersby, so the scribes intended to draw more attention to the inscription.

They did this by hiding literal interpretations of the hieroglyphic messages within obvious puzzles. In other words, the passersby would have to study and reinterpret the hieroglyphic inscriptions. The theory being, as with a rebus, that if the inscriptions were an entertainment, the reader would pay more than passing attention and would work to translate the meaning into plaintext. As years and dynasties passed, the puzzles became more complex, until they reached the point where it was almost impossible to determine the actual meanings. When the inscriptions achieved this level of difficulty, it defeated the original intent (that is, requesting prayers for the deceased), and the practice stopped. Still, it constitutes the earliest recognized cipher.

While they may have been among the earliest to practice secret writings, the Egyptians were not alone among the ancients in hiding their messages in plain sight.

WAX TABLETS AND SLAVE PATES

Credited with being the first historian, Herodotus of Halicarnassus wrote his *Histories* in the fifth century BCE. More storyteller than historian, he related a series of incidents associated with the expansion of the Achaemenid Empire (portions of modern Turkey, Iran, and Iraq). It is full of gossip, fairy tales, legends and small incidents during the wars under a series of kings, culminating in Xerxes' invasion of Greece in 480 BCE.

Herodotus tells a tale of early steganography. A civil war was about to take place, with a general uprising against the Persian rulers of the region. The coconspirators in the rebellion needed a means of communication secure from prying eyes. They turned to the slaves.

They did not trust the messages to paper or tablet, however. Nor did they speak the messages aloud to the slaves. Instead, they shaved the slaves' heads and had the message tattooed on their bald pates. Then, when the hair had grown back, they

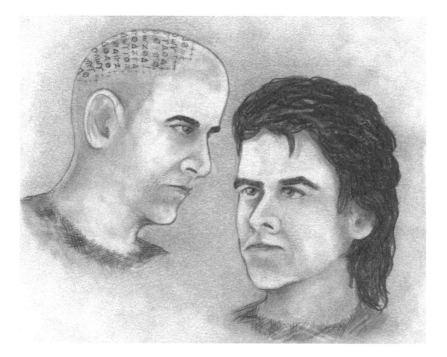

Tattooed Head

When secrecy was more important than speed. A Greek slave's head would be shaved and the message would be tattooed on the bald scalp. When the hair had regrown, the slave would be sent on his way to deliver the message. At the receiving end, the head would be shaved again and the message revealed. (Kismet Images)

sent the slave off on an innocuous mission to another household. There his head would be shaved and the steganographic missive would be revealed. Apparently the messages weren't all that urgent, for the system worked; the Greek uprising was successful in deposing the Persians.

Later, messages were committed to wax tablet. Again it was Herodotus who tells of the attempt of Xerxes I to invade and conquer the city-states of Greece. Learning of the plan, a Greek spy wrote a warning on two wooden tablets. He then covered the writing with a coat of wax. His messengers, when stopped, were able to display the tablets as blank. They appeared to be unused. The messengers were released and continued on their way to Sparta. There the wax was removed, the message revealed, and the Spartans, long noted as the fiercest of warriors of all the city-states, went forth to do battle with and defeat the forces of Xerxes.

Which left Xerxes wondering how the Spartans knew he was coming.

For much of human history, the use of secret writing and codes and ciphers has been associated with divination, magic, and the black arts. It has been looked on as something evil or, at the very least, as something mystic. There has always been something seemingly diabolical in the ability to discern meaning (that is, render into plaintext) from apparent gibberish (ciphertext) or, as in the case of the Spartans and the wax tablets, to read messages that no other can see. It has been likened to the ability to discern meaning from tea leaves or from the liver of a freshly slaughtered bullock or to interpret dreams and omens and portents.

This is understandable. First of all, if you can do it, you don't necessarily want to broadcast the ability. It is, after all, a secret. The last thing you want is for the other side to figure out how you're telling your secrets. They may decide to take action to either read your secrets themselves by intercepting your messages or stop you from doing it in the first place.

It is also true that from a distance and to the uninitiated, many activities associated with the occult or mystic sciences—alchemy and astronomy, to name two common examples—appear to be closely related to the science of cryptanalysis. Arcane symbols and hidden meanings abound in both realms. A string of letters that may seem meaningless at first glance (*abracadabra*) may mean something more, and perhaps nefarious, when placed in the hands of a skilled wizard or under the studied eye of one bent on rendering it into plaintext.

Perhaps it is guilt by association. Certainly those who practiced the ancient arts of divination (or claimed to do so) did not necessarily do so in private. Little glory was to be gained from keeping quiet. The glory was to be had from public divination of the future—and spreading the word that you did it.

The medicine man (or shaman or priest or wizard or pundit) was a person of high status in most societies. And there is something to be said for exalted status, for the respect shown by those around you. The villagers would flock to you with their problems, whether sickness, poor crops, broken hearts, or the enemy's battle plans. It was your council, your wisdom, that was sought and followed. You would be asked to discern the will of the gods or to look into the future to determine the appropriate course of action. You would be asked to reveal what was hidden to those unskilled in the arcane arts. And one who was able to do so, or at least have others think she could do so, would be admired. Perhaps it was in the interpretation of omens, or in the reading of the runes, that status was achieved and maintained. Perhaps it was simply the ability to read the ancient texts, with archaic scripts and strange markings on the page, that showed wisdom and knowledge of hidden things.

In any case, cryptology became muddled—and confused—with magic. It may very well be that this entanglement was aided, at least in the West, with magic's association with the so-called *cryptic scripts*.

The cryptic scripts are termed such because contemporary scholars are unsure of their origins, although there is universal certainty that both were used to transmit hidden messages in times past.

RUNES, OGHAM, AND ARCHAIC LANGUAGES

A little more than 100 years after Herodotus wrote his histories, a new script was making its way across Europe in the form of *runes*, the earliest examples of which date to circa 300 BCE.

The precise origin of the runic alphabet is a matter of some debate among scholars. One theory credits the Goths, a Germanic people who played a large role in the decline of Imperial Rome in the third century CE. But most contemporary scholars trace its development to a derivative of the even more ancient alphabet

Runic Script

This burial marker, replete with runes, stands in a cemetery in Upsala, Sweden. (Photri/Microstock)

first developed by the Etruscans, a civilization populating Italy prior to the rise of the Roman Empire.

In any case, the term is found in Middle High German (*rune,* meaning whispering), Old Irish (*run,* secret) and Old Saxon (*runa,* meaning magician). It is evident that, right from the start, something secret was acknowledged to be associated with this script. Examples are found on weapons and rings and clasps throughout Europe. Some scholars point to the similarity between some runic characters and the contemporary Western alphabet as evidence of a single parent.

It might have been a script of secrets. Just as likely, it was a script of mystical religious sects and secret societies. There seems to be some tenuous connection with the Druids in this regard.

The development and spread of runes across Europe coincided with the fall of Rome. The runic alphabet had its heyday around the first millennium (1000 CE) and continued in use, primarily in northern Europe, until the start of the seventeenth century. This period in southern and western European history, from roughly 400 to 1400 CE, is often called the Dark Ages. Literacy all but vanished with the fall of Rome and the ending of the Pax Romana. The sciences and arts disappeared. What reading and writing was done was kept behind the closed and cloistered doors of monasteries.

Stories and legends surrounding the use of runes included divination and the saying of sooths. Perhaps this is what appeared to have happened. But perhaps the secrets of reading the runes were restricted to the wisest members of the group, and certain powers were ascribed to them solely because they could, in fact, read. It may well be that much of the mystique that surrounded the use of runes arose from the fact that someone could actually read and interpret the scratchings at all.

What is known is that the script expanded from an original set of 28 characters to 33 once it reached the British Isles in the fifth and sixth centuries CE (most likely by invading Saxons).

While this was going on in Britain, almost the opposite was happening in Scandinavia and northern Europe. Changes in the Nordic languages actually reduced the number of characters in the variation of runes used there. The character set decreased to 16 characters, some having two meanings or representing two sounds. It is this character set of runes that was carried by Vikings to Iceland and Greenland, and would have been carried to the New World, had the Vikings in fact made it that far. (As yet, no authenticated rune inscriptions have been found in the Western Hemisphere.)

What is also known with certainty is that runes, in all their varieties, were used for secret writing. At least two different systems, *isruna* and *hahalruna*, have been identified. Both involve the use of a substitution cipher.

The practice of *isruna* divides the character set into three groups, with eight characters in each group. The order in which the character fell was indicated by a series of vertical marks. To translate the message back to plaintext rune, the reader would first determine the group number and then the character number indicated in the message. The secret lay in the grouping of the letters.

Hahalruna also divides the character sets into three distinct groupings. Each character is then represented with a single vertical line, with diagonals moving from the center outward. A single diagonal on the left indicates the first group; the number of diagonals on the right indicate the specific character in that group. Again, the key is in the original grouping of the letters.

The runic system of writing, in all its forms (including as ciphertext and plaintext), had pretty much fallen out of use by the twelfth century, although there are some indications of its use, particularly from northern Europe, continuing into the early seventeenth century. The Christian church, in large measure, was responsible for its eventual decline, as it banned the use of runes in 1639 as one element of its overall effort to put an end to what it considered to be the practice of superstition and magic.

Yet another European alphabet claims a connection with the Druids and things of folklore and magic, although this one more than tenuous. Ogham is a system generally recognized to have been in use from roughly 350 CE until 600 CE and is the oldest form of written Irish.

Much of what we know of the structure and use of the system comes from a medieval text, *The Book of Ballymote*. A single hand-scribed edition exists in the library of the Royal Irish Academy in Dublin. The existing copy is thought to be a fourteenth-century copy of a ninth-century original. It contains a life of St. Patrick, a history of the Jews, stories and genealogies of various clans and kings, and a detailing of ogham.

In the text of the manuscript, we are told that ogham (or ogam, pronounced AH-wam) was developed by Ogma, the Celtic god of eloquence and letters. We are also told that it was a system reserved for the exclusive use of warriors, Druids, and bards of the day, since the common folk were far too simple to grasp its intricacies.

A number of examples, more than 350 carved in stone, survive in Ireland, the Isle of Man, Wales, and Scotland. Nearly all are either property boundaries or tombstones. Unfortunately, many have been defaced, at the direction of the Christian church, it is believed, in an effort to eradicate all things pagan. And since ogham predated the arrival of Christianity to the Emerald Isle and was known to have been used for secret writing, it follows that it was at the very least pagan, if not from the Devil himself.

The script is written both vertically in carved inscriptions (as on tombstones and boundaries) and horizontally in manuscript form. It has 25 characters, each corresponding to a specific sound. Typically, a character will have a center baseline, with a number of strokes radiating from this base.

At least one scholar has argued that these radiating lines suggest the position of fingers or hands and might have been representations of secret signals employed either on the battlefield or by priests during mystic rites. There are also stories of Druids communicating via hand signals, such as a brush across the nose or a certain number of fingers laid against a cheek, which would be represented in ogham. Much of this is conjecture, and it should be remembered that there are reports of leprechauns and something called blarney coming from Ireland too.

It is certain that ogham was used for secret writing, because a number of examples exist and detailed instructions for encipherment are included in *The Book of Ballymote*. What draws the attention is not so much the skill and variety employed in the construction of the various ciphers as the names given to them.

The "point against eye" ogham reverses the alphabet. The "vexation of a poet's heart" ogham mandates the strokes be shortened. The "host" ogham has each letter tripled. The "fraudulent" ogham substitutes one letter with the next in the alphabet. The "outburst of rage" ogham is a substitution cipher. There are a number of others in the manuscript too.

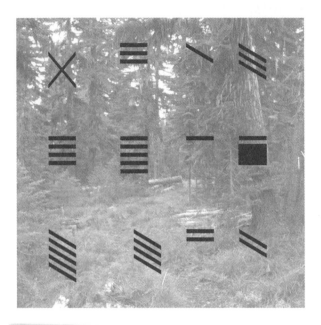

Ogham Text

Typically carved on stone or wood, ogham characters consisted of a series of horizontal, vertical, or diagonal lines or solid squares.

The fall of the Roman Empire marked the beginning of a long period of superstition and ignorance throughout much of Europe. As literacy was stifled, indeed shunned, so was cryptology. There were few advances in the sciences prior to the start of the Renaissance.

There were other civilizations flourishing during the period. And as we have seen, when civilization flourishes, so does the need to tell secrets. Commerce, di-

plomacy, and war all produce secrets in need of telling. The Arab world was experiencing an explosive period of growth and enlightenment. Medicine, mathematics, architecture, commerce, and literature were reaching levels far beyond those in the West. Bound by a religion with strict prohibitions against many forms of visual art, strict adherents turned instead to literature and wordplay. The rebus and the anagram saw a resurgence of interest and development, as did cryptology. Ciphers became commonplace in the palaces and halls of commerce. It has been reported that the system used to collect and record taxes had one of the most elaborate constructions ever employed up to that time.

A number of texts detailing the means and methods of cryptanalysis survive. And these refer to others, now lost, on the same subject. In his monumental book on the subject, *The Codebreakers*, historian David Kahn tells of one such work, *Kitab shauq al-mustaham fi ma'rifat rumuz al-aqlam* ("Book of the Frenzied Devotee's Desire to Learn About the Riddles of Ancient Scripts"), written in the year 855 CE. This work detailed several ancient scripts, including one based on Hebrew characters, and provided instructions for enciphering potions and spells.

All this activity was not limited to areas immediately surrounding the Mediterranean Sea. India and Asia saw the rise of secret-telling as well.

The ancient Chinese first developed their system of pictoglyphic writing in 1300 BCE. While it may have been born like cuneiform and hieroglyphics, its development was significantly different in that it did not develop in the direction of phonics. Rather, the characters representing the syllables have remained relatively constant, while the total number of characters has grown to incorporate new words that came into the language. It was not one that lent itself to ciphers, but it did very well in coding messages. And as already noted, the Chinese had early on discovered the advantages of steganography.

In the Americas, civilizations flourished throughout what today is known as Latin America. The Mayans had achieved a high level of civilization by the time the conquistadors arrived. Their calendars and writings were carved in stone and written on some fairly sophisticated and, for the period, technologically advanced materials.

While their descendants still inhabit Mexico's Yucatan Peninsula and parts of Central America, much of their civilization has been lost. The Spanish invaders

SMOKE SIGNALS

The Great Wall of China, generally acknowledged as a wonder of the ancients, runs more than 4,100 miles across the northern section of the country, snaking across deserts, grasslands, and mountains. Construction began more than 2,000 years ago, before the unification of the country.

Smoke signals. If the weather cooperated, smoke signals could be seen at distances of 20 miles or more. They were used by Native Americans during the eighteenth and nineteenth centuries and by the Chinese circa 200 CE.
(National Archives and Records Administration)

The original intent of the builders was not to create a single continuous wall. (That's a myth, like the common belief that it is the only human-made structure visible from space.) It actually started as a series of isolated structures located on the outposts of various states. The joining of these structures did not begin until the Qin Dynasty (circa 221 BCE).

One of the purposes of the wall was to serve as a defensive line against invading Huns. The other was to provide signaling stations, along which messages could be passed over great distances within a relatively short period of time.

The method of choice was the smoke signal. There is documentary evidence to suggest the common use of smoke signals by the Chinese at roughly the same time that Herodotus was jotting down his histories.

Smoke signals, of course, are commonly associated with Native

Americans during the Plains Wars of nineteenth-century America. Though it is true that they were used then, it is not necessarily true that the method was indigenous to the Western Hemisphere. Scholars believe the methodology was developed independently by societies populating the areas now known as the People's Republic of China and the United States.

The process is fairly simple. An open fire is built (using not-quite-dry wood is best), over which a blanket is placed for a short interval. This allows the volume of smoke to increase. As the blanket is pulled away, a puff of smoke rises. Skilled operators can vary the size and sometimes, if the wind is cooperating, the shape of the smoke that is released.

Smoke signals have the advantage of being visible over great distances—20 miles or more. (Keep in mind that a good day's ride on horseback is about the same distance.) Disadvantages include the weather (a too-windy day is going to cause problems, as will a downpour) and the speed at which the signals can be sent aloft. Using a system like Morse code would limit a station to one or two words per minute. On the other hand, the messages usually weren't long and involved and smoke signals worked quite well.

There is little evidence to suggest that an extensive uniform code was employed. In most instances the sender and the receiver constructed a system for their own, perhaps one-time, use. Anyone within line of sight would be aware of the signals, of course. But the communication was often clandestine, hiding in plain sight once again, and the meanings behind the signals would remain a mystery.

A single puff usually meant "Warning" or "Alert" or "Pay attention"; two puffs often meant "All is well" or "Nothing to report"; and three puffs was a sign of urgency or danger.

An often-used variation would be to build not one fire but a series of individual fires, each

(cont.)

(cont.)

giving off a continuous stream of smoke. Sometimes these would be used as above (one fire for "Alert," etc.). Sometimes a volume of fires would be built to lead the enemy to believe that there were a lot more of you than there actually were (spreading a little disinformation) or leading the enemy to believe your forces were over on that far plateau, when in fact they were sneaking up behind the enemy (a little bit of misdirection).

Smoke signals were an easy system to implement, and they worked reasonably well for thousands of years. They passed into the realm of history only when other forms of secure long-distance communication, such as the telegraph, were established.

destroyed most of the writings and defaced temples and public places in the name of spreading a more advanced European civilization. Unfortunately, few attempts were made to record what was being destroyed. Still, a very few examples of Mayan writings survive. They still have not been completely translated. Progress has been made (it is now understood that their arithmetic was 20-base rather than 10-base, for example), and work continues to bring the fruit of this ancient culture to the twenty-first century.

Nor is Mayan the only extinct script that has yet to be deciphered. The Etruscan language is a mystery. Although the Etruscans populated much of Italy prior to the rise of Rome and thousands of examples of their writings have been unearthed by archeologists, little is known about them. Theirs was a civilization, it appears, that was built on commerce rather than war. While their alphabet has been largely reconstructed, no key has been found to decipher the writings.

Similar examples survive from Crete, from the people known as the Elam of western Iran, and from Northern India. Strictly speaking, work on these scripts is not the work of cryptanalysis, but it does press hard against the boundaries.

Many ancient languages, of course, are well known and documented. Latin, for example, is often called a dead language, in spite of its everyday use in academia, law, and medicine. Ancient Greek, Middle English, and other old languages survive, if not thrive, in the halls of academia.

WINDTALKERS

And some ancient languages have been put to good use by the tellers of secrets. During World War II, the Japanese, who were attempting to penetrate field communications of U.S. Marines, were stonewalled when they intercepted messages of the windtalkers.

It was early 1942, and despite published reports to the contrary, the war was not going well for the Allied powers in either Europe or the Pacific. Hitler's armies had captured most of Europe, were advancing in the Middle East, and were well placed in North Africa. The Japanese had surprised the American fleet at Pearl Harbor, dealing a nearly crippling blow. The island of Guam was overrun. The Philippines were in danger. Across the Pacific, Allied personnel, civilian and military, were being pushed back or simply overwhelmed.

The decision had been made in Washington, after consultations with the other members of what was coming to be called the United Nations, to concentrate on Europe before turning all attention on the Japanese empire.

This was not to say that Japan was to be left alone. Stiffening defensive operations, backed by a stiffening resolve on the home front, were underway. Initial plans called for a series of advances against Japanese conquests in Southeast Asia, in China, and in the islands of the South Pacific.

It would be the United States Marine Corps that would lead the charge. Members of this elite service would bear the brunt of the amphibious invasions and the island hopping. Still more plans were made to get it done efficiently and with minimal loss of life.

Long before the Manhattan Project had yielded its secret weapons in the form of the Fat Man and Little Boy atomic bombs, the Corps unveiled its own secret weapon. So secret was it, in fact, that its existence was not revealed until long after the Manhattan Project and Magic (see pages 186 and 114) were public knowledge.

Philip Johnston paid a call on Major General Clayton Vogel, USMC, in his headquarters at Camp Elliot in California. Johnston, a veteran of World War I and a civil engineer, was the son of a missionary and had spent a great deal of his life on reservations among the Navajo. Living and working side by side with these Native Americans for more than 20 years, he had become fluent in their language.

He knew that Navajo had never developed a written script. No standardized dictionary had ever been compiled. And while the language was an important element of life among the people, rich and flexible in its combination of word groupings, it was virtually unknown outside the isolated communities. Johnston had a remarkable idea. He proposed the formation of a special communications unit, composed entirely of members of the Navajo nation, within the Marine Corps. Their mission would be to provide secure communications on the battlefield.

To say here that there was skepticism about the plan would be an understatement. Prejudices and racism were still very much a part of American society at the middle of the twentieth century. The military services were all segregated; for example, African-Americans in uniform were rarely on the front lines. They could be found performing manual labor, driving trucks, or serving in the officers' mess aboard ship, and they were always under the command of a white officer.

Japanese-Americans, particularly those in the states of the American West, faced worse. They were citizens of the United States, nominally granted the freedoms and protections guaranteed by the Constitution. Still, given little notice, they were evicted from their homes, forced to vacate their businesses, and placed in internment camps. This was the darker side of the home front that was revealing itself in the face of national crisis.

The Plains Wars and the Indian Wars of the Southwest were not dim and distant memories. General Douglas MacArthur, commanding a theater of operations for Allied forces, was the son of a man who had earned renown as an "Indian fighter." Many in leadership position had fathers or grandfathers who still carried the scars of battle inflicted by the Native Americans as they fought to preserve their homes and way of life.

And now the Marine Corps was entertaining the radical idea of enlisting Navajos. A new generation of warriors was proposing to do battle with the white man's enemies. It had been tried before, during World War I, using the Choctaw language, but it met with limited success.

It took some doing, but a demonstration was scheduled to prove the point. A message was given to a Navajo in English. This he translated while speaking, in his native tongue, to another Navajo at the other end of the line. The message was received and given back to the waiting officers. The transmission wasn't an exact word-for-word translation, but the system was new and the messengers were largely untrained, so allowances were made. The point had been proven, and the windtalkers were born.

More than 400 Navajo men participated in virtually every Pacific invasion for the balance of the war. They spoke and served with distinction.

Commanders on the battlefield were enthusiastic. Traditional methods of encoding and decoding messages were cumbersome and took time, something that could not be wasted in the midst of a firefight. But the windtalkers could conduct secure communications in real time; one spoke and the other translated. And there

Windtalkers

Private First Class Preston Toledo (left) and Private First Class Frank Toledo, cousins and Navajos attached to a Marine artillery regiment in the South Pacific, relay orders over a field radio in their native tongue, July 7, 1943. (Photri/Microstock)

A WINDTALKER'S DICTIONARY

When the Marine Corps initiated its windtalker program at the onset of World War II, it found few words in the ancient Navajo language to correspond with military terms. Rather than twist English into Navajo or invent new Navajo words altogether, a system was developed that adapted the traditional Navajo language to English counterparts. In many cases, it was a verbal rebus, using mental images of established concepts to represent then-contemporary usage.

ENGLISH	NAVAJO WORD	LITERAL TRANSLATION
Aircraft carrier	TSIDI-MOFFA-YE-HI	Bird carrier
Amphibious	CHAL	Frog
Armor	BESH-YE-HA-DA-DI-TEH	Iron protector
Artillery	BE-AL-DOH-TSO-LANI	Many big guns
Banzai	NE-TAH	Fool them
Battleship	LO-TSO	Whale
Bomb	A-YE-SHI	Eggs
Bomber plane	JAY-SHO	Buzzard
Cable	BESH-LKOH	Wire rope
Camouflage	DI-NES-IH	Hid
Cemetery	JISH-CHA	Among devils
Coast Guard	TA-BAS-DSISSI	Shore runner
Commanding general	BIH-KEH-HE (G)	War chief
Corps	DIN-NEH-IH	Clan
Craft	AH-TOH	Nest
Cruiser	LO-TSO-YAZZIE	Small whale
Destroyer	CA-LO	Shark
Dive-bomber	GINI	Chicken hawk
Entrench	E-GAD-AH-NE-LIH	Make ditch
Fighter plane	DA-HE-TIH-HI	Hummingbird

HOW TO TELL A SECRET

Flare	WO-CHI	Light streak
Fortification	AH-NA-SOZI	Cliff dwelling
Grenade	NI-MA-SI	Potatoes
Howitzer	BE-EL-DON-TS-QUODI	Short big gun
Minesweeper	CHA	Beaver
Minute	AH-KHAY-EL-KIT-YAZZIE	Little hour
Mortar	BE-AL-DOH-CID-DA-HI	Sitting gun
Mosquito boat	TSE-E	Mosquito
Motor	CHIDE-BE-TSE-TSEN	Car head
Number	BEH-BIH-KE-AS-CHINIGH	What's written
Observation plane	NE-AS-JAH	Owl
Patrol plane	GA-GIH	Crow
Plane	TSIDI	Bird
Planes	WO-TAH-DE-NE-IH	Air force
Platoon	HAS-CLISH-NIH	Mud
Pontoon	TKOSH-JAH-DA-NA-ELT	Floating barrel
Pyrotechnic	COH-NA-CHANH	Fancy fire
Robot bomb	A-YE-SHI-NA-TAH-IH	Egg fly
Rocket	LESZ-YIL-BESHI	Sand boil
Sailor	CHA-LE-GAI	White caps
Scout	HA-A-SID-AL-SIZI-GIH	Short raccoon
Semicolon	DA-AHL-ZHIN-BI-TSA-NA-DAHL	Dot drop
Ships	TOH-DINEH-IH	Sea force
Sniper	OH-BEHI	Pick 'em off
Squad	DEBEH-LI-ZINI	Black sheep
Submarine	BESH-LO	Iron fish
Tank	CHAY-DA-GAHI	Tortoise
Tank destroyer	CHAY-DA-GAHI-NAIL-TSAIDI	Tortoise killer
Torpedo	LO-BE-CA	Fish shell
Torpedo plane	TAS-CHIZZIE	Swallow
Transport	DINEH-NAY-YE-HI	Man carrier
Village	CHAH-HO-OH-LHAN-IH	Many shelter

is no documented evidence that their secure communications were ever breached by enemy forces.

So successful was the experiment that it remained an element, a secret one, of battlefield communications through the Korean War and the Vietnam War. It wasn't until 1968 that the existence of the program was declassified and made public.

The system did pose its own set of problems, however. The first was finding enough men of military age who could speak the language. For several generations at that point, it had been schooled out of them. Use of the native tongue was discouraged in the interests of assimilation, so special schools were opened to teach the men their own language.

A second problem was that the Navajo language had no words for common military terms such as *tank* and *airplane*. Here the flexibility of the language came to the fore. Other terms were substituted. *Tank* became *chay-da-gahi*, or "turtle." And *observation plane* became *ne-ahs-jah*, or "owl."

In short, the Navajo developed a sort of verbal rebus in their communications. Rather than making up new words or spelling out an English equivalent, they used existing words that carried a mental image close to the meaning they were attempting to convey.

In 2001, Congress bestowed its highest honor, the Congressional Medal of Honor, on the original contingent of windtalkers.

CHAPTER 3

Hiding in Plain Sight

Falmouth, Virginia, April 1863

THE ARMY OF THE POTOMAC WAS STUCK IN THE MUD, ENCAMPED on the north bank of the Rappahannock River overlooking the town of Fredericksburg, some 40 miles north of the city of Richmond. It was the midpoint of the American Civil War, although of course those involved didn't know that at the time.

Several months earlier they had made an initial crossing, engineers in blue erecting pontoon bridges while under serious fire from sharpshooters in gray. It was deadly work. But not nearly as deadly as what happened once they got to the other side.

Confederate General Robert E. Lee and his Army of Northern Virginia were waiting on the heights just beyond the town. Lee had positioned his army well behind entrenchments and with a clear line of fire. Advancing on that field came wave after wave of Union troops under the command of General Ambrose Burnside.

Marching in disciplined formation straight into the face of Lee's massed artillery and infantry, nearly 13,000 Federal troops died that day, while the Confederates lost more than 5,000. The death count totaled a staggering 18,000 American lives.

As he watched all the carnage on the field before him, Lee turned to one of his corps' commanders, General James Longstreet, and said, "It is well that war is so terrible, lest we should grow too fond of it."

So the Army of the Potomac retreated across the river. They had tried another crossing, downstream this time, but a winter storm caught them and turned them back, wet and cold and miserable. That excursion became known as the Mud March. Seemed the army had walked all over Virginia before winding up back where it started. Morale in the North, not just in the army, wasn't high.

Falmouth, a little unincorporated town on the north side of the river, just across from Fredericksburg, became the winter home of the Federal army in Virginia. And here it was April and they were still stuck in the mud, trading potshots, tobacco, and coffee with their counterparts just across the way.

President Abraham Lincoln relieved General Burnside of command and replaced him with "Fighting Joe" Hooker. Lincoln had also issued his Emancipation Proclamation in January of that year. Lincoln's proclamation started to filter through to the South, and many slaves still in bondage stole themselves from their plantations and headed north to freedom. *Freedmen*, they were called by some. The lawyers termed them "contraband of war."

One such freedman is known to history only as Dabney. His story was recorded in 1889 by Frank Moore in a volume titled *The Civil War in Song and Story: Anecdotes, Poetry, and Incidents*. According to Moore, Dabney had been a field hand on a farm on the other side of the river, and he came through the Union lines with his family, eager for work. He brought with him, too, a keen intelligence and good working knowledge of the topography of the region.

Attaching himself to the army, he became a cook and personal servant to a detachment of Union officers. In the course of his duties, he was exposed to, and fascinated by, the army's use of telegraph and semaphore for communications. Through observation and persistent questioning, he picked up the basics of the signaling systems and soon became adept, to the surprise of the army.

Dabney's wife, meanwhile, also found employment. She was on the other side of the river, in Confederate territory, attached as a servant to a local "secesh" family.

In the course of her duties, she came into frequent contact with highly placed Southern officers who would visit that family's farm just across the way.

For much of their history in the Colonies and later in the United States, African-

Americans in general, and servants and slaves in particular, were largely ignored by those around them. It was almost as if they were invisible, and it was common for white folk to speak freely in their presence, as if they were not there. As a result, they became privy to plenty of information. That was certainly the case with Dabney's wife.

Soon after she started working across the river, the Union officers noticed that Dabney seemed to know quite a bit about Southern plans and the disposition of their forces. General Hooker would learn of the enemy's intentions within hours of their discussion. The information came from Dabney, and it always proved to be correct.

In his book, Moore reports that Dabney never left his post, was never absent from his duties, and couldn't possibly be moving back and forth across the river to collect the intelligence. There was a mystery here, one that needed solving.

When pressed, he revealed his source: his wife.

Taking a small contingent of officers to a small hill outside headquarters, he pointed out a farmhouse across the river, just on the outskirts of the town. That, he explained, was where his wife was working. Next to the house was a clothesline. And on that line hung the tale:

"That clothes-line tells me in half-an-hour just what goes on in Lee's headquarters," he said. "You see my wife over there, she washes for the officers, and cooks, and waits around and as soon as she hears about any movement or anything going on, she comes down and moves the clothes on that line so I can understand it in a minute."

"That gray shirt is Longstreet, and when she takes it off it means he's gone down about Richmond. That white shirt means Hill, and when she moves it up to the west end of the line, Hill's Corps has moved upstream. The red one is Stonewall. He's down on the right now, and if he moves, she will move that red shirt."

An entire system of signals and symbols had been developed between the two, and it was paying dividends to the army. At one point, there was quite a bit of movement on the clothesline telegraph, with shirts shifted and repositioned . . . some moved and some removed altogether.

"It don't mean nothing," Dabney reported. He suggested that the Confederate maneuvers be ignored altogether.

He pointed to a pair of blankets that had been pinned together at the bottom in addition to the top. "That's her way of making a fish trap. And when she pins clothes together that way, it means that Lee is only trying to draw us into his fish trap."

The system remained in place and provided effective intelligence throughout the month of April. In early May, Hooker moved the army in a well-coordinated plan to squash Lee's army. However, when the two armies met at Chancellorsville in northern Virginia in early May, the Army of the Potomac suffered yet another significant defeat, losing 17,000 Union soldiers. In addition to Union losses, the Army of Northern Virginia lost some 13,000—killed, wounded, missing, or taken prisoner. The total was nearly 30,000 Americans, including Confederate General Thomas J. "Stonewall" Jackson.

During the Civil War, one of the most effective intelligence operations conducted on behalf of the Union was centered in Richmond, Virginia, and headed by Elizabeth Van Lew. "Crazy Bet," she was called by the residents of the city. She had lived there most of her life, and when, at the onset of the war, she showed Northern sympathies, she was shunned by her neighbors. She accepted and encouraged her reputation for eccentricity by wandering the streets of Richmond, head cocked to one side as she hummed aloud or held loud and lengthy conversations with nonexistent people. But it was all steganography. Long before anyone had codified the practice of tradecraft and cover, Crazy Bet was a master of it. Her cover was that she must have been crazy to act as she did. No one who was a spy, after all, would call attention to herself by loudly proclaiming the enemy's cause. People ignored her.

Most of the people in Van Lew's network were African-Americans: slaves or freed slaves who did the menial work in and around the Confederate capital. They were allowed to come and go, almost as they pleased, with rarely a second thought. As couriers of secrets, they were in an ideal position. No one would take the time to dig through baskets of vegetables full of dirt and fresh from the fields or to inspect the inside of muddy shoes for the secret messages conveyed there. And since they were servants and laborers and treated as invisible by those who weren't, they came to know a lot about plans and goings-on in the Confederate seats of power.

In what was perhaps one of her more audacious moves, Crazy Bet arranged for one of her freed slaves, Mary Elizabeth Bowser, to be employed by the household of Confederate President Jefferson Davis. Historians disagree as to whether Ms. Bowser provided much in the way of practical intelligence, but after the war Generals Benjamin Butler and Ulysses Grant paid tribute to her.

SLAVES' SIGNALS

There is a long and strong tradition among African-Americans of using steganography. The acts associated with keeping secrets from the masters were dangerous, somewhat enticing, and probably necessary for survival. One such tradition, passed on orally, deals with the use of quilts to convey instructions and directions to runaways, guides of a sort, for the Underground Railroad.

The tradition holds that specific symbols would be incorporated into the otherwise merely decorative designs of the quilts hand-stitched by plantation slaves. These symbols would inform the initiated as to directions to go, places to avoid, and things to do as they made their way to freedom.

It is just a theory, however intriguing it may be. And controversy does surround it. Virtually no documentation exists to confirm the oral traditions that speak of this particular form of pictography. The lack of documentation may be explained by the need for secrecy at the time coupled with the low levels of literacy among the slave population.

An examination of the quilts themselves might help substantiate the theory. Unfortunately, few quilts carrying the supposed symbols survive. Years and decades of hand-washing in harsh lye soap would have destroyed any evidence that may have existed. Still, the oral tradition stemming from former slaves and their children is compelling. But oral tradition, like memory, can be unintentionally embellished and distorted. There might indeed have been a system of directions displayed in the pictograms of the quilts, but without solid evidence, we just don't know with certainty.

Yet we do know that the Underground Railroad was a growing concern in the years leading up to the Civil War. Some historians estimate that upwards of 50,000

FOLLOW THE DRINKING GOURD

The Underground Railroad in the United States was a system that came into being in the early decades of the nineteenth century. Through it, thousands—some say tens of thousands—of slaves made their way to freedom in the Northern states.

It was a dangerous undertaking, and an industry developed around the business of catching and returning fugitive slaves to their Southern owners.

There were strict prohibitions in the South against educating the slaves. They were not allowed to learn to read, for example. The fear among the Southern whites was that the slaves would start to get ideas about freedom, along with the means of making that happen. Despite these prohibitions, however, slaves were well aware that freedom was to be found in the North. And from childhood onward, they were told that North lay in the direction of Polaris (the North Star). And Polaris lay in the handle of the Big Dipper or, as it was known in that day and in that community, the Drinking Gourd.

Federal law at the time required that runaway slaves be returned. The Underground Railroad was an attempt to circumvent the slave-catchers and the law. It is estimated that during the Civil War, more than 500 people circulated throughout the South providing slaves with instructions for the safest route to avoid capture. It was done through song, with people memorizing lyrics.

Peg Leg Joe was an itinerant carpenter who visited plantations in the Deep South and taught one such song to the slaves. Within its lyrics are coded instructions for an escape route from Mississippi and Alabama along the banks of the Tombigbee River. Always following "the drinking gourd," the slaves were told to watch for markings of a left foot or a peg foot that would appear, like graffiti, on the trunks of trees (these would distinguish the main river from branches flowing into it). When an escaped slave reached the point where the Tombigbee merged with the Ohio River, help would be waiting to cross that last river and reach freedom.

FOLLOW THE DRINKING GOURD

Follow the drinking gourd!
Follow the drinking gourd.
For the old man is awaiting for to carry you to freedom
If you follow the drinking gourd.
When the sun comes back and the first quail calls,
Follow the drinking gourd,
For the old man is awaiting for to carry you to freedom
If you follow the drinking gourd.
The riverbank makes a very good road,
The dead trees will show you the way,
Left foot, peg foot traveling on,
Following the drinking gourd.
The river ends between two hills,
Follow the drinking gourd,
There's another river on the other side,
Follow the drinking gourd.
Where the great big river meets the little river,
Follow the drinking gourd,
The old man is awaiting for to carry you to freedom
If you follow the drinking gourd.

Slave Quilt Symbols

According to oral tradition, the designs incorporated into quilts made by African-American slaves gave direction to fugitive slaves escaping to freedom in the North. This reproduction is on display at the National Cryptologic Museum in Maryland. (National Cryptologic Museum)

people made their way to freedom before the onset of the war. And there is solid documentation that suggests these people were guided by the use of symbols, placed like graffiti, along trails in the woods.

"Follow the Drinking Gourd" (see sidebar, page 65) is one example of the documentation. The lyrics of the song contained a code that speaks of these symbols. They would be carved on fallen logs or tree trunks along the route as markers, telling the runaways that they were on the right path. The symbols would be placed by members of the Underground Railroad, secret agents, as it were, who would travel throughout the South enticing and helping slaves to freedom.

THE HOBO CODE

The use of graffiti to convey information, secret or otherwise, is nothing new. Nor is it confined to North America. Archeologists have found it on the interior walls of the Great Pyramids in Egypt. And the excavations of Pompeii, buried by volcanic ash in 79 CE, have uncovered numerous examples of graffiti.

More recently, early-twentieth-century America witnessed a form of graffiti that came to be known as the hobo code. This was a form of secret writing, with a series of symbols that conveyed specific meanings to its initiates.

It actually started in the waning years of the nineteenth century when legions of the unemployed (or seldom employed) took to the road. It was a time of transition in America. The largely rural population of the country was confronted by the challenges that came with the Industrial Revolution. The power of steam had been harnessed, and with this new source of energy came technologies and significant shifts in cultural and social norms.

The economy was changing rapidly. New jobs were being created in the factories that were built in the cities. And the labor pool was expanding with an influx of immigrants from Europe and newly freed slaves migrating north. The skills required to compete successfully for these new jobs were alien to many who had grown up in small-town America. As a result, many were forced to look for work beyond the traditional boundaries of farm and field.

The railroads helped to provide a solution. The tracks that spanned the continent eased the flow of commerce between major population centers. It was along these miles of tracks that the hobos, as they came to call themselves, roamed in their quest for better times and better places. Jobs were scarce and money was tight, and not all could afford to be paying customers. A solution could be found in hopping a freight—that is, climbing aboard a train when no one was looking and taking a ride for free.

Hobo

Which way, 'bo? Hobos hopping a freight in a train yard during the Great Depression.
(Library of Congress)

There are several theories concerning the origin of the term *hobo*. One traces it to Hoboken, New Jersey, a major East Coast railroad hub during the late nineteenth and early twentieth centuries; freight trains moving toward all points of the compass could be hopped there. Another theory claims *hobo* was a contraction of the phrase *hopping boxcars*. A third, and perhaps the most likely, theory places it as a contraction of the term *hobohemian*, meaning an itinerant artist or musician.

It was a lifestyle not suited to the faint of heart. Jumping onto or off of a moving train is dangerous in itself. The railroads employed guards who were instructed (and were often none too gentle) in the ways of preventing the practice. Then, too, most cities and towns had ordinances against vagrancy.

Twentieth-century American pictoglyphs

During the years between the great wars of the early twentieth century, legions of the unemployed (or seldom employed) took to the open road. Some were looking for work. Some were looking for adventure. Some were just looking. These hobos, as they came to call themselves, developed a language of symbols. Scrawled in chalk or charcoal on sidewalks, fence posts, or the back of street signs, it was a code that gave their compatriots a shorthand review of the territory. (Kismet Images)

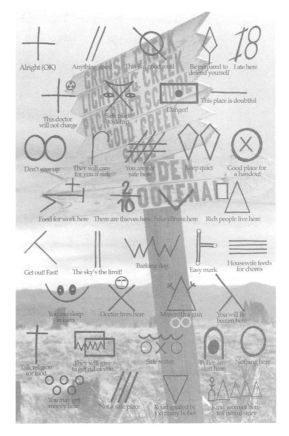

WARCHALKING

The early years of the twenty-first century witnessed new activity known as wardriving. It consisted of those who were searching for a wireless connection to the Internet—through a trademarked technology called Wi-Fi—driving aimlessly around city blocks seeking their connection. If they could connect, they'd found a hot spot, a locale that allowed users to log on to the Internet without being plugged into anything.

In June 2002, a group of wardrivers were discussing the state of Wi-Fi and one of them was reminded of the hobo code. The decision was made to create an updated version of the code. Symbols were designed that night and were posted on a blog (a Web log) the next day by Matt Jones, complete with instructions and a downloadable document depicting the new icons. Jones's blog is well read and respected, so the icons were an instant and international hit.

The system was dubbed *warchalking*. And the icons began to appear, written in chalk or charcoal, on walls and sidewalks and signposts to designate hot

Still, thousands of men—and women—took to the open road. Some were indeed looking for work. Some were looking for adventure.

Hobo jungles were informal meeting places, campsites set up just outside the watchful eyes of the local railroad and police forces. Here the hobos would congregate, sharing whatever food, stories, and directions they had. Entrance would be gained through a traditional greeting—"Which way, 'bo?"—which acted as a password into their world.

And it was here that the signs and symbols of the hobo code would be updated and communicated. Actual meanings and the physical marks varied somewhat, depending on the region of the country. In effect, there were various regional dialects

spots to the initiated. To the uninitiated, these—like the hobo code itself—were just random marks.

The icons became so popular so quickly that commercial enterprises began to incorporate them into their advertising and promotional materials. Some reportedly went so far as to begin drawing the symbols themselves to identify hot spots within their cafés.

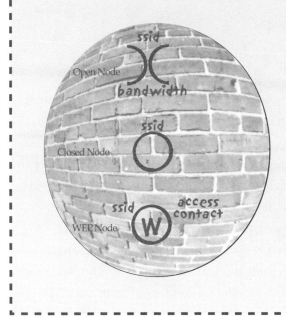

Open Node
ssid
bandwidth
Closed Node
ssid
WEP Node
ssid
access
contact

Warchalking. A digital-age version of the Depression-era hobo code, warchalking employed three distinct symbols scrawled on sidewalks or the side of buildings to alert the initiated to the presence of a Wi-Fi hot spot. By providing such information as the bandwidth available and the SSID (the network's name), the symbols allowed laptop computer users to log onto the Internet without actually plugging any wires into anything. The system originated in London but quickly spread throughout the world as the information was distributed on the Internet. *(Kismet Images)*

of the same language. And the symbols changed as local populations became aware of their existence and meanings and would use this knowledge to lead the hobos astray . . . or at least astray from them.

But the system did exist, coming to fruition during the years between the great wars of the early twentieth century. The Great Depression was upon America and most of the world. Those trying economic times greatly expanded the ranks of the hobos.

Using chalk or charcoal, the symbols would be scrawled on signposts, on sidewalks, on billboards, under railroad bridges, and along highways. They provided a shorthand review of the terrain. To those initiated in their meanings, these graffiti-like signs would warn of dangers or point in the direction of handouts and safe passage.

The ranks of the hobos thinned considerably with the coming of World War II and the jobs created by war industries. There was now work to be had, and many considered a regular meal and a warm bed to be a fair trade for an unencumbered life on the road. But while the number of full-time hobos dwindled, as a subculture they did not disappear entirely. Communication between them has evolved with technology, with e-mail, Web sites, and blogs replacing visible graffiti.

URBAN GRAFFITI

Which is not to say that clandestine communication via graffiti has disappeared—quite the contrary. It can still be seen every day, particularly on the streets of larger cities.

As was the case in ancient Pompeii, or even more ancient Athens, much of the graffiti seen today consists of obscenities and vulgarities. Usually scratched or spray-painted on walls, subway cars, and bridges, most can be dismissed as uninteresting (for our purposes) acts of vandalism—not all.

The discerning eye will see other messages in the writing on contemporary walls. Scholars are now beginning to study the various forms of graffiti that appear in urban areas, particularly the large metropolitan centers of southern California (Los Angeles, San Diego), the northeastern United States (New York, Boston, Philadelphia, and Washington, D.C.) and middle America (Chicago, St. Louis, Kansas City), and patterns are beginning to emerge.

Like the hobo code of previous generations, there are meanings associated with many of the signs and symbols to be found. And as with the hobo code, these meanings shift from city to city—different dialects of the same language. But to the initiated, the meanings become apparent.

Perhaps the most prolific and visible form of contemporary urban graffiti is that of *tagging*, or writing one's name in a stylized fashion in as many public places as is possible. By its nature, of course, it is not clandestine. The purpose is exactly the opposite of clandestine: to be noticed, by as many people and as often as possible. For this reason, tagging appears on the sides of trains, subway cars, and buses, in addi-

tion to walls and schoolyards. The more ubiquitous, the better; the more elaborate—with stars and swirls and shadows and slashes—the better still. But the aspect that commands the most respect is the seeming inaccessibility of the venue. Writing one's name on a wall is one thing, but writing one's name in letters four feet high on a billboard hanging over an eight-lane highway is the mark of someone noteworthy.

Somewhat more covert is the category of graffiti that began to appear with the emergence of the large organized street gangs of the late 1960s and early 1970s.

While tagging is an individual activity, the other forms of "gangland" graffiti are not. Often highly elaborate and covering physically large spaces, these often start with the name of the gang, again done in a stylized manner. They are used to demarcate that particular gang's territory or to boast of the gang's superiority. Though its purpose is to alert the reader to the presence and the power of the gang, this graffiti's manner and the style, in addition to its overt statements and symbols, carry meaning.

For example, Latino gangs as a general rule employ more flamboyant and stylized lettering, complete with varying colors, drop shadows, and embellishments, whereas African-American gangs employ a simpler stick or squared block letter style. At a glance, therefore, the ethnic makeup of the gang would be apparent.

Gang Graffiti

The Crips gang of Southern California will often use highly stylized hands to announce their specific gang. Represented here are the 46th Street Crips and the 90th Street Crips. Crossing out another gang's name is considered a mark of disrespect. Among most gangs, the stylized arrow next to the name denotes a claim to this specific turf.

Specific symbols are often employed. Use of a chicken or a duck implies disdain for another group. Arrows indicate supremacy over a neighborhood or a neighboring gang and are an open challenge to members of the rival gang. In Los Angeles, use of a pit bull is always associated with the Bloods; the Crips on West Boulevard

Tagging

The objective of tagging is to have your moniker, your "tag," seen by as many people as possible. Putting it on a cross-country boxcar is one way of achieving the objective.

use a stylized version of the Warner Bros. logo. In all cases, defacing another gang's graffiti is the ultimate sign of disrespect and is an open challenge.

The use and symbolism within gang graffiti is evolving. Many of the styles and symbols that were evident in the closing years of the twentieth century are shifting. Perhaps it is only natural as an art form spreads throughout a culture, the norms and standards become more relaxed until they dissipate.

TATTOOS

Such is certainly the case with skin art. Tattoos, at least in Western cultures, once were intended to convey specific messages to those with an insider's knowledge.

Although the practice of adorning oneself with stylized art and design is ancient, it is only in relatively modern times and in relatively modern cultures that specific images were intended to convey specific meanings.

It was the mariners of the eighteenth century who introduced tattoo symbols to the Western world, specifically those sailing with Captain Cook to some of the farthest edges of the world. The story goes that these men encountered the art among the natives of the South Pacific and decided that tattoos would be an efficient and distinctive way of letting others know that they'd been around the world. Living in the hold of a wooden sailing ship for long sea voyages was uncomfortable enough. There wasn't a lot of room for your person. And there certainly wasn't a lot of room for your personal belongings. So, the theory goes, rather than buy a souvenir at some exotic port—something that would have to be stowed in an already too small space—sailors chose to have their mementos tattooed to their skin.

It was these sailing men who first began to codify the symbols to be employed. The anchor on the forearm, for example, came to mean the sailor had crossed the Atlantic Ocean. A full-rigged sailing ship indicated the wearer had made the crossing from the Atlantic to the Pacific oceans by sailing around Cape Horn at the southern tip of South America. A golden dragon denoted a crossing of the international date line. A braided rope around the wrist said the wrist belonged to a deckhand.

The system wasn't confined to the typical British tar. One estimate said that during World War I, more than 90% of American sailors wore at least one tattoo.

Nor were tattooed symbols confined to the more salty members of the population. Circus sideshows had featured "The Tattooed Lady" or "The Tattooed Man" since their inception in the mid-1800s. The first commercial tattoo parlor in the United States was established in San Francisco, in 1846.

But commercially available tattoos rarely carried hidden meanings. The symbols and images had obvious meanings and were designed to be seen and admired as physical adornment. It wasn't until the late 1960s, when various groups began to adopt body art as a way of identification, that hidden meanings began to appear.

Among prison populations, for example, specific images became identified with specific meanings, as with the sailors of an earlier day.

A spider's web tattooed on an elbow or shoulder originally indicated that the wearer had killed someone. This later evolved, so that the number of rings in the web stood for the number of years the individual had spent behind bars. A variation placed a spider in the web, the spider taking on the meaning of the killer.

A teardrop tattooed under an eye originally had the same meaning as the spider web. Among Latino prisoners, this later shifted to indicate the loss of a loved one or family member while the wearer was incarcerated (prisoners weren't supposed to cry, so the teardrop indicated their sorrow).

As was the case with graffiti, the meanings have dissipated with the popularity of tattoos. A spider web today may just mean that the wearer happens to like the design. Indeed, most contemporary tattoo designs are selected by the wearer in

ESSENTIAL TO THE WAR EFFORT

Among the events triggered by the attack on Pearl Harbor in December 1941 was one of the largest booms that the tattoo industry had seen to that point. It wasn't that young men were flocking in to get tattoos. Rather, it was that young men were flocking in to get tattoos fixed.

In 1909, the United States Navy had issued a recruiting regulation stating, "Indecent or obscene tattooing is cause for rejection. The applicant should be given an opportunity to alter the design, in which event he may, if otherwise qualified, be accepted."

At the onset of World War II, there were many tattoos out there that the navy would have deemed indecent and/or obscene, and since the navy was choosing to stick by this particular regulation, tattoo parlors around the country did a booming business by covering up the potentially offending displays.

Naval recruiting centers were inundated with applicants sporting tattooed images suitable for service during a real shooting war. There were butterflies and bubbles covering images that were somewhat earthier. Ladies newly clad in full-length skirts adorned biceps and forearms. Flowers and fans were strategically placed aboard fighting ships at sea.

Charlie Wagner was generally

the neighborhood tattoo parlor from commercially available prefabricated sheets called "flash." Each flash has upwards of 20 images ready to be applied. The meaning, if any, is usually personal and has to do with an important event or element in the wearer's life. It can be a favorite musical act, the street where he (or she) grew up, or just an attractive design. The use of Asian characters may mean that the person is devoted to peace or just that the person likes the way the character looks.

acknowledged to be one of the premier tattoo artists of the day, operating out of his studio in New York City's Bowery. At one point early in the war he was hauled before a judge to answer a charge dealing with the city's sanitary code. His defense was that he was performing "essential war work" in his parlor by covering all the nudes. Without his services, he reasoned, the navy would be deprived of the services of many otherwise fully qualified men. The country needed the navy. The navy needed these men. Charlie was therefore essential to the war effort. If we truly wanted total victory in the Pacific, Charlie had to keep doing what he had been doing.

He got off with a $10.00 fine.

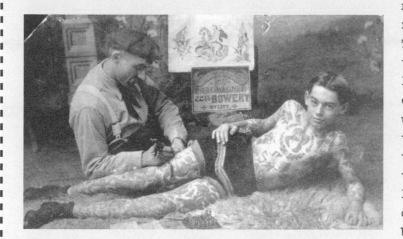

Charlie Wagner, operating out of a studio in Manhattan, was generally acknowledged to be one of the premier tattoo artists of the day. His work was deemed essential to the war effort during World War II. *(Tattoo Archive)*

And there are fads. A tribal band around the biceps was a popular motif during the 1990s. Few, if any, have been inked during the first decade of the twenty-first century.

The very notion of tribal bands underscores two important points in this business of secret-telling, particularly secret-telling in public places. The first is the idea of inclusion versus exclusion. By being part of a group or a team or a gang, the individual gains status in the form of respect—self-respect and respect from those who wish they too were part of that group. The second is the feeling of being "in the know"—that is, having an insider's knowledge of what is really going on.

SECRET CLUBS AND DECODER RINGS

Both elements were successfully employed during the middle years of the twentieth century by programmers and marketers who developed and broadcast popular entertainments on the radio aimed squarely at adolescents.

Little Orphan Annie, for example, was a character first made popular through the Sunday comics of American newspapers. Her adventures continued on the radio, and listeners were able to participate through special clubs. Club members would identify themselves to one another through secret handshakes and could distribute secret messages through the use of her decoder rings (available when you sent in two cereal box tops).

1935 SECRET WIG WAG SIGNS

1. When you touch your right ear with your thumb keeping your fist closed tight, it means—"See me in private —I have important news!"

2. Tapping your lips with the first two fingers of your **left** hand means—"Silence —an outsider is listening and trying to discover our secrets!"

3. When you cross your two fingers in front of you (like the keys are crossed on your pin) it means "Tonight is Club Night"—listen for a secret radio message from Annie.

Little Orphan Annie's Hand Signals

A member in good standing of the Little Orphan Annie Secret Society in 1935 was required to know the secret password ("leaping lizards") and an elaborate series of secret signals. (Hake's Americana)

TOM MIX

It was a ritual among certain members of the population.

Every weekday afternoon at exactly 5:45, radios across the country were tuned to the NBC Blue Network (which later became ABC). It was the height of the Great Depression in America. If you had been lucky enough to be in the right place, you'd see, in a semicircle around the Philco brand radio in the living room, every kid in the neighborhood.

It was the daily meeting of the Ralston Straight Shooters of America. And they were gathered to listen to the latest installment of a series of "thrilling, exciting mysteries" (self-proclaimed) starring none other than Tom Mix and Tony the Wonder Horse.

Thomas Hezekiah Mix (1880–1940) really was a cowboy before becoming one of the early stars of Saturday morning movie serials. He also served a stint as the town marshal of Dewey, Oklahoma. Fame came to Tom, and Tony, during a movie career spanning 26 years, when he made 336 feature films (most of them silent), and the 15-chapter serial *Miracle Rider*. With the advent of the "talkies" (that is, movies with sound), Tom looked for other opportunities, joined the circus, and started touring.

It was early in the Great Depression that the Ralston Purina Company was seeking a vehicle to reach their target audience: kids. They approached Tom with an idea. They'd like to produce a daily radio program around Tom's

Logo of the
Tom Mix Ralston
Straight Shooters.
(Kismet Images)

Tom Mix and Tony
the Wonder Horse.
(Kismet Images)

The Official Decoder Membership Badge. About 2 ½ inches high by 1 ½ inches wide and made of pressed metal, it was a simple mechanical device. A rotating pistol on the front pointed to the secret message on the back. *(Kismet Images)*

How to Use Your Official Decoder MEMBERSHIP BADGE

With your official membership decoder badge it's easy to decode secret radio messages INSTANTLY. You need not write anything down. There's nothing to remember.

Each symbol on the badge stands for a secret word. For example, the word HEART stands for TOMORROW—GUN means WATCH FOR—DAGGER stands for CLUE, etc. To find the secret word just point the gun on the back at the symbol. The arrow on the back of the badge will then point to the secret word.

How to Decode a Secret Message

When a secret radio message is read over the air LISTEN for TWO things:— (1). THE NAME OF A PERSON and (2). A SECRET CODE SYMBOL. DISREGARD EVERYTHING ELSE. For example:

Secret message: JOHN WEARS AN ANCHOR ON HIS WATCH CHAIN
Decoded means: JOHN — GUILTY
Secret message: JOHN HAS A KEY TO THE RANCH HOUSE
Decoded means: JOHN — INNOCENT

If the NAME OF A PERSON DOES NOT APPEAR in a secret message, then pay attention ONLY TO THE CODE SYMBOL. For example:

Secret message: I SAW A STAR TONIGHT
Decoded means: DANGER AHEAD
Secret message: THERE'S LIGHTNING IN THE SKY
Decoded means: YES

When TWO SYMBOLS appear in the message, use both. For example:

Secret message: A COWBOY WEARS A GUN NOT A DAGGER
Decoded means: WATCH FOR CLUE

REMEMBER: LISTEN ONLY FOR SECRET SYMBOLS AND NAMES OF PERSONS. PAY NO ATTENTION TO ANYTHING ELSE. With a little practice you can use this secret code in talking with other Straight Shooters and no one will know what you're saying.

PAGE 12

SYMBOLS AND SECRETS

Heart	Danger ahead
Pistol	Yes
Knife	No
Anchor	Beware of
Star	Innocent
Lightning bolt	Tomorrow
Skull	Watch for
Horseshoe	Clue
Key	Guilty

The secret manual provided instructions to members of the Ralston Straight Shooters of America for decoding the messages broadcast during each day's program. *(Kismet Images)*

continuing adventures. An actor would impersonate Tom, so he could keep touring. The deal was done, and on September 25, 1933, the *Tom Mix Ralston Straight Shooters* were on the air. It became one of the most popular juvenile series of its day. And its day lasted from 1933 until 1950.

Arguably, one of the most popular and successful characters to employ secret clubs and messages and decoder badges was Tom Mix (see sidebar). First as a circus star, then as a star of movie serials, and finally as the star of a daily radio broadcast, Tom Mix (the man and the character) became the prototypical cowboy hero. His

An important part of the experience was forming a Straight Shooters'
Club right in your own neighborhood. Just by sending in box tops (from
Ralston cereals, of course), you could get everything you'd need.

Sales of Ralston breakfast cereal skyrocketed. Box tops came flying
into Ralston's St. Louis headquarters, and free premiums went flying back out across the country. Guns, rings, books, lariats, coins,
bandanas . . . all carried the Tom Mix Ralston Straight Shooters'
brand.

And, of course, the secret decoder badge. The badge was perhaps
the most important piece of all. You needed it, and you would hound
your parents to buy Ralston so you could get it. Because every day
the broadcast would end with a message for the Straight Shooters of
America. A coded message. You simply had to have the badge to get the
message straight.

Along with the badge came the *secret manual*. This came with the ad-
monition to keep the book in a *secret place*, for it contained all sorts
of confidential information on the *secret salute*, the *secret handshake*,
the *secret password*, the *secret knock*, the *secret whistle*, and the *secret
flashlight signal*. It also told you how you could get more paraphernalia
by sending in more box tops. Incidentally, it also had the instructions for correctly deciphering the daily message.

Hundreds of thousands of these premium items were distributed. Today they are highly prized collectables.

The Tom Mix Ralston Straight Shooters didn't make the jump to television in the 1950s. But Tom Mix is not gone. There are Tom Mix mu-
seums in Dewey (where he had served as marshal) and Mix Run,
Pennsylvania (his birthplace).

celebrated exploits, purely fictional of course, set the standard for latter-day superheroes and did much to promulgate the myth and mystique of the "code of the
West." He was good looking. He played by the rules. He stood for general "good-
ness" when he fought the bad guys. And along with his horse—Tony the Wonder

Horse—he always got the girl (an advantage that the younger members of the group didn't always appreciate).

His adherents were called the "Ralston Straight Shooters," and the youth of America were invited to join the group (again, by sending in cereal box tops). When they did, they received an instruction booklet along with their decoder badge, initiating them into the codes, signals, secrets, and ways of Tom Mix–dom.

An important aspect of being a Straight Shooter was the ability to decode the secrets broadcast every afternoon. During the show, a secret message would be given. Across America, decoder badges would swing into action, and all real Straight Shooters (that is, those who had sent in the box tops) would gain an insider's knowledge into what was really being said.

The tradition of broadcasting very public displays of very private information continues in the realm of professional sporting events, particularly football and baseball games.

SIGNALS IN PROFESSIONAL SPORTS

Before the start of every play, as the quarterback steps up to the line of scrimmage, he surveys his surroundings. As master of the field of play, it is his responsibility to set the play in motion, but only after he has satisfied himself that all is as he wishes it to be. He takes note of the defense he faces, of where the linemen and linebackers have positioned themselves for the play. He checks his own team to make sure that people are where he wants them to be. He glances at the clock to see how much time he has remaining before he must start the play (he usually has about 10 seconds or so at this point; things are moving pretty fast). Then he sets himself over the center and begins to shout his game plan for his team, the other team, the spectators in the stands, and those watching at home to hear. The man is telling you what is about to happen. But you need to be initiated into the code to understand what he is really conveying.

A short time earlier, the quarterback has received a secret message from his coach. Since the 1990s, a radio receiver has been standard equipment for a quarterback's helmet. It is a one-way affair; he can receive but he cannot send. Through the earpiece built into the helmet, he can listen to his coach's instructions as to the next play. Television cameras will often catch a coach on the sidelines giving the play, but he will usually have a clipboard or a piece of notepaper held before his mouth, hiding his lip movements from prying eyes.

According to Brian St. Pierre, a professional quarterback who has played with the Pittsburgh Stealers and the Baltimore Ravens, there is an unspoken agreement throughout the National Football League (NFL) that the coach's transmissions will not be intercepted by the opposing team. And the system usually works pretty well, although some teams have noticed that the transmissions are often garbled or experience some technical difficulty when they're playing on the road. This doesn't seem to happen when they're playing in their own stadiums.

Once he has received the play from the sidelines, the quarterback takes his team into a huddle. There, in the middle of the field, he tells the team of the plan: the play, their formation, and the count on which the ball will be snapped.

After the huddle breaks, and as he surveys the field while his side is getting ready, he will glance almost casually at his receivers, particularly at the one he intends to receive the coming pass. There is steganography involved here, for the quarterback has to be careful not to give any indication (1) that he may be planning to pass or (2) to whom he may pass. It is usually nearly impossible for the average spectator, even one who knows what to look for, to see what is happening. The quarterback will look at all the receivers by sweeping his eyes across the field. If all goes well, he will see all without revealing that he has seen anything. This, according to St. Pierre, is something that is practiced.

Prior to the game, the quarterback has met with his receivers and worked through a special set of signals. If the receiver flexes his fingers in a certain way or adjusts his helmet or shakes his foot before planting it, he may be telling his quarterback not to go ahead with the original plan because he is being covered in such a way that the play may not work, or he may be telling his field general that all is well. Either way, it will be a quick, seemingly random motion.

When he finally gets up to the line, some two or three seconds later, he begins his cadence. The calling of signals originated with the Yale football team of 1882.

But it was legendary Notre Dame coach Knute Rockne who is credited with putting a system in place in the 1920s so that the signals called meant something other than just when the ball would be snapped.

Brian St. Pierre

Quarterback with the Baltimore Ravens of the National Football League. As field general of a professional football team, he tells secrets throughout the game. (Courtesy of the Baltimore Ravens)

Before going into his count, at the start of every play the quarterback will yell something along the lines of "Green 52! Green 52!" That changes virtually every week, with colors and numbers carrying different meanings on a weekly basis. In most cases it means nothing. It is steganography, a cover to hide the times when it really does mean something. For if the signals received from his receivers or the formation he faces from the defense are not to his liking, the quarterback will change the play right there on the line of scrimmage. It is called "an audible," and it will happen perhaps two or three times in any given game.

This week, "Green 52" may mean nothing. This week, "Blue 84" may be the code for an audible. Next week, "Blue 84" may mean nothing, and "Green 52" may be the audible signal.

From the time a field referee calls a halt to one play, by blowing his whistle to signal that the ball is "dead," the offensive team has 24 seconds to get themselves together and start the next play. During that 24-second period, there are several sets of clandestine communications taking place on the field. If you know where to look, there's almost as much going on between the plays as there is during the plays.

That is certainly the case with major-league baseball. To a casual observer, the game consists of a pitcher winding up and throwing the ball, hopefully past the batter, to his catcher behind the plate. Occasionally someone will hit the ball and there will be a lot of running around out in the field. But all that is just the obvious, overt, part of the game. There is also a clandestine game taking place. Signals are flying and secret messages are being conveyed across the diamond to players on both sides. Lots of covert activity to be seen, if you know where to look.

Perhaps the most visible, the signals broadcast most often via television coverage, are the hand signals given by the catcher to the pitcher. The catcher will flash one, two, or three fingers; perhaps against his right or left thigh. He's calling the pitch. He is telling the pitcher that he wants him to throw a fast ball, inside. The pitcher will sometimes shake his head indicating that he wants to throw something else. The catcher will then flash a new sign until there is harmony between the two. The batter, of course, isn't supposed to see or know any of this. But just in case one of the batter's teammates happens to see and attempts attempts to convey the information, the signals between catcher and pitcher are changed on a regular basis. So it cannot be said with certainty that one finger laid against the right thigh means a fastball low and in-side. It may mean that, of course. But it may be a call for a curve.

There are other signals too. Before the pitcher throws the ball, particularly if there are runners on base, he will glance at the

Baseball Signals

Keyote, mascot of the Carolina League's Frederick Keys AA baseball club, demonstrates the third-base coach's signals. You may want to bunt now. Or not. (Kismet Images)

runner ostensibly to satisfy himself of the runner's posture and position. Ostensibly. He's also looking for a signal from his teammate covering that base. A tug on the belt or a spreading of the fingers may be a signal to throw the ball to the base in an attempt to tag the runner out (the runner isn't supposed to see or understand this).

It is a signal that has been agreed on before the start of the game by the pitcher and his infield. It is out there in the open for all to see, like the hobo code or a piece of graffiti, but only the initiates understand the meanings.

While all this is going on, the members of the infield are swapping signals too. They too are clandestine and will consist of seemingly random motions: a scratching of the arm, adjusting of a cap, a kick in the dirt. They're mapping strategy in case of a hit or a base runner's attempt to steal his way to the next base. These are all signals developed and practiced before the start of the game.

At least as interesting as all the signals flying around the infield are the gyrations of the third-base coach. He will go through a series of motions, and he's not at all shy about them. He will clap once, perhaps twice or three times. He will grab his cap. He will slap his forearm. He will drag his palm across his chest. He will tug on his ear or scratch his nose. Then he may clap yet again.

The third-base coach is giving instructions to the batter. Every motion means something, but only one will be the instruction for that particular pitch. He may be telling the batter to hit away or to bunt. And that may change with the next pitch, depending on the pitch just thrown or the position of the base runner(s) or where an infielder happens to be standing. The key to breaking this code is in knowing which motion is the actual instruction. It could be the third movement. It could be the one right after he tugs his cap. It could be contained in the number of times he claps his hands at the end of the series of movements. When he rubs his hand across his chest, he could be telling the batter to take a called strike or he could be telling him to forget everything up until that point and start over with the signals.

Just as in the NFL, there is an unspoken agreement among the major-league baseball teams to not try to read the other team's signals. And if those signals are somehow read and decoded, to not transmit that information to the players on the field. All this is made more complicated when players move between teams. The agreement extends to the players; they should not be asked to tell the secrets of the teams they just left, nor should they volunteer the information. Still, all these signals are changed on a regular basis.

So there is a reason for the long pauses between pitches. There's a lot to do out there. The batter doesn't just need to knock the dirt from his cleats; he also needs

to see what he's supposed to do next. Besides, there's quite an extensive conversation taking place in the infield. As is the case with pro football, there's arguably as much action taking place between plays as there is when the ball is in play.

ARMY SIGNALS IN THE FIELD

That actually isn't too much different, at least in this respect, from what is experienced by an army in combat. An army's time in the field has been called long stretches of boredom separated by short periods of intense terror. And while it may indeed be a bit boring for the troops at grunt level, those higher up are engaged in solving the problems of planning and logistics.

The American Civil War, for example, lasted 1,458 days. Of these, only 120 saw major battles where significant forces were engaged. Between those battles, both armies were occupied in shifting positions, trying to find something to eat and just passing the time while in camp.

Both sides would go into winter quarters when the weather started to turn foul in the late fall. The soldiers would construct elaborate dwellings, with carefully laid-out streets, street signs, and even town squares for their camps.

The problems of communication between headquarters and individual units were simplified while in camp. Runners and adjutants would be sent, sometimes with scrawled orders, to find unit commanders. And with the street system in place, the commanders weren't all that hard to find.

It was not so easy in the field. Units would be scattered across miles of terrain, and they were not often stationary, which further complicated the ability of couriers to deliver timely orders and reports. The telegraph could be used on occasion, and both North and South had the equipment and expertise to string temporary lines. But this was not often a practical solution.

Much more common was the use of semaphore. This was a system that employed signal flags by day and lanterns by night to convey complex messages over long distances. It was, in effect, an optical form of the telegraph. The position of the flags (or lanterns) would determine the letter of the alphabet to be transmitted.

The Semaphore Alphabet

As depicted by a World War II-era U.S. Navy technical manual. (Kismet Images)

The system was hardly revolutionary during the American Civil War. Nearly 100 years before, an installed network in France included more than 550 stations and covered nearly 3,000 miles. That system had been put in place during the French Revolution in the 1790s. There was an obvious and urgent need for swift communication between the central government and outlying regions, particularly since the government was surrounded by enemies—internal and external.

It was expensive and it was cumbersome. Messages sent by waving flags could be sent only a relatively short distance (the distance at which you could see a flag) and were hampered by hills, trees, and bad weather. Direct line of sight between stations was mandatory. Still, when it worked, it worked rather well. The trick was to have enough stations on hilltops and high above the tress, and trained operators to staff them, to catch a message and send it on.

This principle was put into effective practice during the Civil War. The original pioneering attempts were developed during the 1850s by the army's Major Albert Myer. His system was based on Morse code, with the movement of flags roughly corresponding to the dots and dashes otherwise transmitted by fixed wires. It was well established at the onset of the war. In fact, both Confederate and Union armies employed semaphore communications during the Battle of Bull Run, the first major confrontation of the war. It was called "wig-wag" because of the positioning of the flags.

Civil War Semaphore Station

Located on high ground just outside Sharpsburg, Maryland, this semaphore station was staffed by members of the Signal Corps during the Battle of Antietam, September 1862. (National Archives and Records Administration)

Aided by spotters armed with binoculars, troopers of the U.S. Army communicated with semaphore during the Plains Wars of the late nineteenth century. (National Archives and Records Administration)

It is a fairly simple technology and is still in use, both for civilian and military applications. Nautical signal flags are a derivative of early semaphore. So are the red, green, yellow, and checkered flags used during auto races, and the storm flags used by the National Weather Service.

Those uses, of course, are not intended to be clandestine. During time of war, the signals are encrypted so that even if they are spotted by the enemy (highly likely), they won't necessarily be correctly interpreted.

Another type of signal is the whistle. The chief benefit of a whistle is its piercing high-pitched tone. Not only is it distinctive, but it carries a long way.

BLIMEY ! I CAN READ THAT SIGNAL ALRIGHT.

British World War I-era comic postcard. (Kismet Images)

Old Salts knew this well, and made ample use of the device, for it could easily be heard above the howls of a storm. While individual codes varied between ships, somewhat like regional dialects, certain basic calls (such as the one calling for attention: a one-count low tone followed by a two-count high tone and a two-count low tone) were standard. Contemporary hiking trail guides also use a standard system. A single blast simply means "stop and wait." Two blasts mean

"Stop and come here." Three blasts mean "Stop what you're doing and come here *quickly.*"

There is but one essential element in the conveying of clandestine information through open signals, regardless of whether the signals are flags or graffiti or the scratching of a nose or a spider web on an elbow or a red shirt hanging at the end of the line. The essential element is that you (the good guys) know what it means, while they (the bad guys) don't.

CHAPTER 4

The Devices of Secrecy

Moscow, August 1945

ANEW DAY HAD DAWNED. PEOPLE AROUND THE WORLD WERE celebrating. The war was over.

There are conflicting figures and the true count will probably never be known, but most historians place the number of casualties resulting from World War II at a nearly incredible 78,000,000 men, women, and children. Every continent bore the marks of the war's brutality. And the statistics that are still being compiled some 50 and 60 years later tell a story that must never be forgotten.

It was a war unlike any other in recorded history in many respects. It was a mechanized war, one that saw rapid and terrible advances in the technologies of killing. High-altitude bombing and long-range artillery allowed for mass destruction of property and persons without the killer actually seeing his victims. The armies of the world, locked in their struggles, certainly inflicted death and destruction on one another with grim and determined efficiency.

But the fact remains that fully 65% of the war's dead were noncombatant civilians. They were victims of bombings, of disease, of starvation, of systematic attempts at annihilation, and of being caught in combat zones.

The figures detailing casualties of World War I are still in dispute, but the total is placed somewhere near 22,000,000 men, women, and children with the bulk, 80% or more, being combatants. World War I was called the "war to end all wars" at the time, but technology had advanced between the wars.

The generation of Europeans born during the 1880s and 1890s called themselves "the lost generation" as disillusionment with humankind set in following their grim experiences in the trenches. Perhaps they earned that title. But if so, what title do we bestow on the men of the Soviet Union born in 1923? Less than 20% of Soviet men born that year survived to see August 1945.

So August 15, 1945 was a day of celebration, a day of relief. It was V-J Day. Representatives of the Empire of Japan formally surrendered to the forces of what was

Sir Winston Churchill

The Prime Minister of Great Britain during World War II. (National Archives and Records Administration)

coming to be called the United Nations on the deck of the battleship *Missouri* in Tokyo Harbor. Japan was the last of the Axis nations to surrender. The war was finally over.

At least that was the official story.

The real story was that while one war—a hot and shooting war—was just ending, another war—the Cold War—was just getting under way.

Winston Churchill called it the Iron Curtain and said it had descended across the face of Europe, splitting Communist East from democratic West. As most of Europe, indeed much of the world, lay prostrate following the shooting war, the great powers—principally the Soviet Union and the United States—stared at one another across a bargaining table and waited for the other to blink.

George Patton

General George ("Old Blood and Guts") Patton advocated rearming the German army after World War II and advancing on Soviet forces. (National Archives and Records Administration)

THE OFFICE OF STRATEGIC SERVICES

William J. Donovan, "Wild Bill" as he was called (but not to his face), had been a personal friend of Franklin Roosevelt long before Roosevelt became president.

Donovan was a decorated hero of World War I. And between the wars he had undertaken a number of unofficial fact-finding missions on behalf of the United States. He had traveled to both Europe and Asia, supposedly on business, but actually taking note of military developments. His missions were unofficial because (1) Donovan was a private citizen without affiliation with any branch of the government, and (2) such missions were technically illegal at the time.

As war became imminent, Roosevelt asked Donovan to prepare a document outlining an office that would gather and provide analysis of the information and intelligence that was coming to the government in the form of reports from overseas diplomatic missions, from allied nations, and from the military.

In preparing the document, Donovan retreated to his home in the Georgetown section of Washington, DC. There he was joined by William Stevenson, Winston Churchill's official liaison to the United States for all intelligence matters. Stevenson (who later became famous with the publication of *A Man Called Intrepid*) and a naval aide worked with Donovan to draft the proposal. It would outline the scope of the mission, the use of paramilitary forces, the training facilities required, the new agency's structure, budget and administrative needs. In short, it pretty much outlined the whole of the new Office of Strategic Services. There was some haggling and give-and-take with the

FBI and the Pentagon regarding some of the details, but the essential elements of the proposal were adopted as submitted. Cryptology

Once it was established by presidential decree, Donovan got the credit and assumed overall direction of the OSS. The secret behind it all is how much William Stevenson and his aide contributed to the document. They never received public credit, of course. It wouldn't be good politics to announce that the British were pretty much behind the U.S. efforts in clandestine activities. Besides, Stevenson was attempting to keep a low profile for obvious reasons.

Stevenson's aide was also an interesting man. He was a commander in the Royal Navy by the name of Ian Fleming. After the war, Fleming went on to be a successful novelist. *Chitty Chitty Bang Bang* was one of his books. But he is perhaps best known for another series and its main character . . . Bond, James Bond.

Once it was established by presidential decree, Donovan got the credit and assumed overall direction of the OSS. The secret behind it all is how much William Stevenson and his aide contributed to the document. They never received public credit, of course. It wouldn't be good politics to announce that the British were pretty much behind the U.S. efforts in clandestine activities. Besides, Stevenson was attempting to keep a low profile for obvious reasons.

Stevenson's aide was also an interesting man. He was a commander in the Royal Navy by the name of Ian Fleming. After the war, Fleming went on to be a successful novelist. *Chitty Chitty Bang Bang* was one of his books. But he is perhaps best known for another series and its main character . . . Bond, James Bond.

There are quite a few secrets still to be told about this period of history (many won't be declassified for some years to come). But some facts are well known.

First of all, there were elements among the civilian and military leadership in the United States that wanted to continue the war against the Soviet Union after the Nazis had surrendered. General George Patton advocated this position. He actually spoke of rearming the German army and turning it around to face the Soviets. Cooler heads prevailed.

For their part, as trusted allies and recipients of billions of dollars of Lend-Lease support from the United States, the Soviets nonetheless remained suspicious of the United States. Even while the war was under way, the Soviets had placed spies within the establishments of Great Britain and the United States. When, during the Potsdam Conference, President Harry Truman tried to advise Soviet Chairman Joseph Stalin of the existence of a working atomic bomb, he was surprised that "Uncle Joe" showed so little reaction. The reason was that Stalin already knew. His scientists had been getting regular reports of nuclear weapons development from deep within the supersecret Manhattan Project. And while the Soviets hadn't yet mastered the new technologies involved, they weren't far behind in duplicating the results.

The West didn't know this at the time, although it was soon to find out.

Seal

The Great Seal of the United States, presented to Averell Harriman, U.S. ambassador to the Soviet Union, by the children of Moscow in 1945. A listening device hidden within went undetected for more than six years while it hung in the ambassador's private office in the embassy. (National Cryptologic Museum)

There were a number of things that the United States didn't know. One was that a new kind of war was about to begin. In its rush to downsize the military and cut government spending, it was entering the Cold War with one hand tied behind its back: The OSS, the independent agency of intelligence-gathering and analysis and of cloak-and-dagger operations, was being disbanded.

Created at the beginning of World War II to gather and coordinate all the information flowing into federal offices from a variety of sources, diplomatic and military, the OSS had performed remarkably in all theaters of the war. But now it was considered redundant. Its mission had been completed. And its duties were being divided between the State Department, the Federal Bureau of Investigation (FBI), and the Pentagon. (The Pentagon, in particular, didn't really want any of the OSS resources, since it already had rival intelligence operations working for the navy and the army.)

It was in August 1945 in keeping with the spirit of celebration and camaraderie that followed the end of the war, the schoolchildren of Moscow, in a very public show of goodwill, presented a special gift to Averell Harriman. Mr. Harriman, the ambassador of the United States to the Soviet Union, received the children and the gift with the spirit with which it was purported to be given.

It was a beautiful thing, actually: the Great Seal of the United States carved in wood. Attached to its handsome plaque, it measured roughly 24 inches across. As a thoughtful gift, and as an attractive decoration, it was most appropriate hanging on the wall of the ambassador's private office. And there it stayed, from that day in 1945 until the day in 1952, when the listening device hidden inside the seal was finally discovered.

A passive device had been hidden inside a cavity within the seal. The microphone was activated only by radio waves sent from a van parked on the street outside the embassy. The device was virtually undetectable. For six years, the Soviets were listening to every conversation that took place inside the ambassador's private office.

The use of state-of-the-art technologies and mechanical means of transmitting secrets is hardly new. Commercial and military endeavors have always placed priority on secure communications, and employment of cutting-edge technologies, whatever the era, is a matter of course.

COURIER DEVICES

Perhaps the first mechanical device developed for transmission of secrets was the skytale of the ancient Greeks. It was a simple device, but effective for its day and time.

The Greek historian Thucydides described its configuration and use by the Spartans in the fifth century BCE. It started with an officer's staff. A strip of parchment or cloth would be wound tightly around its length. Then, in plaintext, the message would be written.

The parchment would be unwrapped, and the empty spaces would be filled with meaningless characters. Thus, if intercepted, the message would appear to be gibberish.

The parchment containing the message would be sent by courier to the recipient, where an identical officer's staff would be produced and the parchment would be rewrapped. The message would appear. Not a bad system, as long as your officers carried different staffs than did their officers. It did have the decided benefit of plaintext. Neither code nor cipher was required to keep the message secure.

Another system with the same benefit also used plaintext hidden in plain sight. The sender would write an innocuous-looking letter, full of news and gossip and,

Skytale

The ancient Greeks would wind a strip of cloth around a baton and write their message. When the cloth was unwound, empty spaces would be filled with null characters. It was only after the cloth was rewound around an identical baton on the receiving end that the message would become clear. (Kismet Images)

perhaps, a weather report. If it were to be intercepted, prying eyes would not give it a second glance. This, of course, is one of the objectives of secret writing. If it were not sent on its way, at the very least it would be ignored.

A second courier, however, would carry a custom mask. It would be a template placed over the document. The intended, and secret, message could be read through the holes. It was cumbersome in that two couriers would be required for

Secret writing during the American Revolution.

Sir Henry Clinton, in command of British troops in the Colonies, wrote an innocent-looking letter to his subordinate, General John Burgoyne (Figure 1). By separate courier, he sent a mask (Figure 2). When the mask was placed over the letter (Figure 3), the real message in the form of secret writing was revealed. (William L. Clements Library, University of Michigan)

successful transmission (for if a single courier carrying both the plaintext document and its mask were to be intercepted, the plan would be transparent). The couriers would travel at different times and along differing routes to their single destination. When it worked, it was effective.

The system was used during the American Revolution. Sir Henry Clinton was commander-in-chief of British forces in the Colonies at the time. A letter survives that he wrote to a subordinate general, John Burgoyne, in 1777. At first reading, it appears to be a note informing Burgoyne of Clinton's move to Philadelphia, a fact that had already been accomplished. But when a mask is placed over the letter, the true message appears: one about the movements of a British force (the bulk of Clinton's troops, actually) down the Chesapeake Bay. It is not information that any of the generals would have wanted in the hands of the rebels. At that point Clinton was sitting in Philadelphia with a small force, while the Continental Congress had been forced to flee westward to York, Pennsylvania and Washington and his men were north of Philadelphia. Clinton would have found himself in an uncomfortable position had his weakness been known. But as it was, Clinton's letter got through to Burgoyne.

ENCRYPTION DEVICES

Thomas Jefferson designed one of the more ingenious and enduring cipher devices. Jefferson developed a small machine, roughly six inches long, which allowed the user to quickly and easily encode a message. The machine consists of a set of 36 independent gearlike wheels, each with an individual number and joined on a central shaft. All are held together with a metal clasp. The alphabet is printed, in random order, around the exterior edge of each wheel.

When a message is to be rendered in cipher, it is spelled out in plaintext using the alphabet printed on the wheels' exterior edges. The message at that point is plainly visible. The user then simply picks another row of letters and sends this as the code. Upon receipt, the recipient arranges the wheels on his device to the same order as the coded message, and then examines the other rows to find the plaintext message.

The device is so simple to use, and the resulting encryption is so secure, that

JEFFERSON'S DEVICE

The National Cryptologic Museum is located just outside the gates of the most private of all public agencies, the National Security Agency (NSA), in Fort Meade, Maryland.

Historians, curators, and scholars populate the museum's staff. Permanent and rotating exhibits display artifacts crucial to a cor-

rect understanding of the history of cryptology, with an emphasis on American efforts. Entrance to the museum is free to the public.

On a pedestal under Plexiglas in the middle of the museum's main exhibit floor is an item that appears to be Jefferson's device. The museum claims it does not have documentation to prove the provenance of the device, but it is believed to be Jefferson's.

Jefferson's Cipher Machine. This may or may not have been the cipher device designed by Thomas Jefferson; the curators at the National Cryptologic Museum at Fort Meade in Maryland cannot say with certainty. *(National Cryptologic Museum)*

the military used the device, with minor variations, for the better part of the twentieth century; the U.S. Navy still uses it.

Although Jefferson designed the device, there is no evidence to suggest that he ever actually used it. Totally different, and less secure, ciphers were used while he served as secretary of state and later as president. In fact, he even instructed Meriwether Lewis in the use of a different cipher prior to his famous trek with William Clark.

Jefferson's motivation for developing the device has never been determined.

THE VIGENÈRE TABLEAU

Named for Blaise de Vigenère, a sixteenth-century French cryptologist, the Vigenère tableau provides multiple alphabets for encryption of a message.

The plaintext letters are the top row; the key letters are the first column on the left side. Using the key, ciphertext letters are substituted for plaintext.

```
    a b c d e f g h i j k l m n o p q r s t u v w x y z
A   A B C D E F G H I J K L M N O P Q R S T U V W X Y Z
B   B C D E F G H I J K L M N O P Q R S T U V W X Y Z A
C   C D E F G H I J K L M N O P Q R S T U V W X Y Z A B
D   D E F G H I J K L M N O P Q R S T U V W X Y Z A B C
E   E F G H I J K L M N O P Q R S T U V W X Y Z A B C D
F   F G H I J K L M N O P Q R S T U V W X Y Z A B C D E
G   G H I J K L M N O P Q R S T U V W X Y Z A B C D E F
H   H I J K L M N O P Q R S T U V W X Y Z A B C D E F G
I   I J K L M N O P Q R S T U V W X Y Z A B C D E F G H
J   J K L M N O P Q R S T U V W X Y Z A B C D E F G H I
K   K L M N O P Q R S T U V W X Y Z A B C D E F G H I J
L   L M N O P Q R S T U V W X Y Z A B C D E F G H I J K
M   M N O P Q R S T U V W X Y Z A B C D E F G H I J K L
N   N O P Q R S T U V W X Y Z A B C D E F G H I J K L M
O   O P Q R S T U V W X Y Z A B C D E F G H I J K L M N
P   P Q R S T U V W X Y Z A B C D E F G H I J K L M N O
Q   Q R S T U V W X Y Z A B C D E F G H I J K L M N O P
R   R S T U V W X Y Z A B C D E F G H I J K L M N O P Q
S   S T U V W X Y Z A B C D E F G H I J K L M N O P Q R
T   T U V W X Y Z A B C D E F G H I J K L M N O P Q R S
U   U V W X Y Z A B C D E F G H I J K L M N O P Q R S T
V   V W X Y Z A B C D E F G H I J K L M N O P Q R S T U
W   W X Y Z A B C D E F G H I J K L M N O P Q R S T U V
X   X Y Z A B C D E F G H I J K L M N O P Q R S T U V W
Y   Y Z A B C D E F G H I J K L M N O P Q R S T U V W X
Z   Z A B C D E F G H I J K L M N O P Q R S T U V W X Y
```

Vigenère tableau

As **an example**, let us encrypt *meet me tonight* using *secret* as the key word.

First we will find the *s* in the key column, and then run our finger along that row until we come to the column with the first letter of our message *(m)*. The ciphertext character is found where the column and the row meet. In this example, the ciphertext character is *e*. Repeating the process, we produce the following:

PLAINTEXT MESSAGE	KEY	CIPHERTEXT MESSAGE
M	S	E
E	E	I
E	C	G
T	R	K
M	E	Q
E	T	X
T	S	L
O	E	S
N	C	P
I	R	Z
G	E	K
H	T	A
T	S	L

Without the key word, the ciphertext message (EIGKQXLSPZKAL) is indecipherable. Since this tableau uses multiple alphabets, a single character in the ciphertext may stand for a single character in the plaintext (see *L* in our example), or it may not (see *K* in our example). Using a key phrase (such as *come retribution*) rather than a key word (such as *secret*) makes the message all the more secure.

Had he intended to use it, perhaps, in clandestine communication with his protégé James Madison, during the contentious election of 1800? Or afterward, when Madison became his secretary of state? Did they actually use it? Or was it merely an intellectual exercise? We will probably never know with any degree of certainty.

It wasn't until 1922, when references and a detailed description of the device were rediscovered among his papers in the Library of Congress, that the existence of the device was even known. It was about that time, by sheer coincidence, that the military adopted the use of an almost identical device, this one developed independently.

It is not surprising that Jefferson dabbled in cryptology, since he dabbled in so many things—architecture, philosophy, political science, agriculture, education, music, and commerce. Nor is it surprising that he would try his hand at invention.

The late eighteenth and early nineteenth centuries saw an explosion in the world of invention. These were inventions that would have profound impact on society. Eli Whitney's cotton gin (*gin* being short for *engine*) received its patent in 1794. Robert Fulton's steamboat, although hardly the first ever designed, received a patent and proved commercially viable during its trips on the Hudson River in 1807. And steam-powered locomotives drove the railroads into becoming the growth industry through the middle part of the century.

Invention flourished in the world of cryptology as well. One German scholar, Dr. Siegfried Tuerkel of the Criminological Institute of the Vienna Police Department, made a study of crypto-machines. Working at about the time of the rediscovery of Jefferson's invention, he counted 196 patents from six countries on machines to encode documents. Fully one quarter of these patents were issued in the United States. Many were far too simple to provide truly secure communications; others were far too cumbersome to be of practical value. But some of the best minds of the nineteenth century, including Charles Babbage (credited with the creation of the first computing machine) worked on producing systems of cryptology.

Many were based on the system originally proposed by Blaise de Vigenère some 200 years earlier, which rotated through a series of ciphers based on a single keyword.

In its original form, the system was quite good and nearly indecipherable using the tools readily available at the time. But it was also complicated. And few wanted to invest the time required to create the cipher or to translate a message back to plaintext. So a watered-down version was propagated, and this is what was used by many of the devices.

It was certainly used in midcentury by military elements of the Confederate States of America. It was dubbed *le chiffre indéchiffrable* ("the indecipherable cipher") at the time and hailed as the last word in the field. The Confederates employed at least two different devices during the war designed to be used with Vigenère: one a cylinder, the other a brass disk.

In theory, it should have worked well. In practice, however, the resulting messages often seemed to have confused the Confederates more than they confused the Federals. As it turned out, Confederate commanders rarely had operators in the field who were skilled at encoding or decoding missives.

In the war department, right next to the White House, President Lincoln had

BOOTH'S TRUNK

Historians generally agree that John Wilkes Booth, although showing Southern sympathies, acted on his own in putting together his various plots to kidnap and, later, assassinate Abraham Lincoln. There is no hard evidence to suggest that he was in communication with officials within the government of the Confederate States of America, or in their pay as an agent or spy. And certainly Jefferson Davis and other members of the Confederate cabinet publicly deplored Booth's actions after the fact.

On the other hand, it is a matter of historical fact that on the day after the assassination, when Booth's belongings in the National Hotel in Washington, D.C. were examined, a curiosity was discovered at the bottom of his trunk: the Confederate Vigenère tableau, which was identical to the one found in the office of the Confederate Secretary of State, Judah P. Benjamin.

This has never been fully explained.

John Wilkes Booth is tempted by Satan to kill President Abraham Lincoln in this contemporary broadside. Historians agree that most likely, Booth acted as a free agent without instructions from Richmond. Still, an examination of his belongings after the deed was done uncovered the secret Confederate cipher. *(Library of Congress)*

three men—David H. Bates, Albert B. Chandler, and Charles A. Tinker—all just barely out of their teens, who displayed an absolute genius when it came to ciphers. They were the primary telegraph operators of the war department. From varying backgrounds in telegraph offices and general commerce before the war, these men brought a variety of skills to their assignment. Lincoln spent a good deal of his presidency in their office (it was on a desk in their office that he wrote the Emancipation Proclamation), reading dispatches as they came in from the field.

For most of the war, the South used only a very few key phrases with their system: *MANCHESTER BLUFF* and *COMPLETE VICTORY* for most of the war, and *COME RETRIBUTION* toward the end, when it appeared all was lost.

Because the war department telegraph operators had broken the Confederate codes and were able to read Southern messages with ease, Lincoln and his generals were often as well informed as President Davis and his generals in Richmond.

COMINT (communications intelligence—information gained from breaking into the opposition's communications) is certainly a desirable thing, although it had little impact on the battlefield and did little to hasten the end of the Civil War. In his *Memoirs,* Ulysses Grant noted that "it would sometimes take too long to make translations of intercepted dispatches for us to receive any benefits from them. But sometimes they gave useful information."

JAPANESE PURPLE AND GERMAN ENIGMA

Useful information, on the other hand, is an understatement for what the Allies received from COMINT during World War II. The Purple encryption system used by Japan during the war in the Pacific and the Enigma-based systems used by the Axis during the European war had both been compromised early. The difficulty wasn't so much in reading the messages and getting vital information but in deciding exactly what to do with the information received. Too liberal a use might alert the enemy that their communications were being read.

Japanese communications had been breached first. At the end of World War I, American planners had seen Japan as a threat to stability. Their navy was growing, and their army had made inroads to Manchuria and was threatening a general invasion of China. Concentrated efforts were being made to crack their systems of codes and ciphers.

The Japanese naval codes were very good. And the United States at the time was sorely lacking in ability to crack them because few Americans were fluent in Japanese, schooled in military disciplines, and eligible for a high-security clearance. But at least as big a problem was the level of encryption used by the Japanese. The codes were secure, not only in transmission but also in physical location. None were known to be anywhere other than on warships, in offices in Tokyo, and in the wholly inaccessible Japanese embassy. The big break came during a party. An American naval officer who had been assigned to keep tabs on his Japanese counterparts, and who had become rather chummy with them, attended that night. Apparently one of the partyers revealed that a copy of the Japanese navy's operational code was actually on American soil. Here was intelligence pointing to a copy in the office of a vice-council, off embassy grounds.

Further investigations revealed that the vice-council was actually a spy, an officer in the Japanese navy assigned to intelligence-gathering duties in the United States. Late one summer night in 1920, American intelligence officers arrived at the vice-council's office, after hours and without an appointment. Not long afterward, a photographic copy of the codebook was housed in the Office of Naval Intelligence (ONI) in Washington, D.C.

The official designation was JN-1, since it was the first Japanese naval code to be read. By the time of the attack on Pearl Harbor, a little over 20 years later, ONI was reading JN-25, the twenty-fifth version of the naval cipher. Those familiar with the operation referred to it as "red code" because the binder that held the photographic prints of the codebook was red.

The Japanese never knew. They believed throughout the war that their various signals were secure, particularly since they had switched to a mechanical system of encryption in 1931. And that mechanical system was a problem.

Not only had the ciphers changed but also the complexity had been magnified many times over. Just how many times, well, ONI wasn't sure. They had never seen the machine, and they didn't know where to begin. They honestly didn't know how much they didn't know. They needed to get their hands on one of those machines, but that was unlikely.

In Washington, the machine was in the hands of Captain Tamon Yamaguchi, Japanese naval attaché. His apartment-office was in the swanky Alban Towers at the junction of Wisconsin and Massachusetts Avenues, just a few blocks from the Naval Observatory and in the heart of the embassy district. It was an elegant address, which added to Yamaguchi's consternation with the electrical problems.

On an intermittent basis, his lights would begin to dim, flicker, and then go dark. Minutes later, before he could do anything about it, they'd come back on. It was irksome, but not enough so that he'd want to move. He really just wanted it fixed.

On a July evening in 1935, Captain Yamaguchi and his wife attended a party at the home of a friend, an American naval officer. The party was part social, part diplomatic. It was to be on the occasion of *chugen*, a traditional Japanese midsummer festival. Yamaguchi brought most of his aides, except for a chauffeur and his yeoman-code clerk.

During the dinner the two aides left to run the office and again experienced the power outage. This time it lasted longer than a few minutes, so they angrily summoned the building's electricians. Two men arrived, dressed for the job and with the tools of the trade in hand. They proceeded to give the apartment a thorough going-over. By flashlight, they went from room to room, tracing wires and seeking the short circuit. Their examination was very thorough. They were no more or less thorough when they got to the code room. It was by flashlight that they were able to examine the machine, along with the partially completed message the yeoman had been transcribing. The short circuit had been found, and fixed, in another room. Everyone was happy.

The power interruptions, of course, had been staged. The electricians were ONI personnel. They knew what they were looking for, and they knew it when they saw it. It was on the basis of the information they gathered that night that ONI specialists were able to begin the monumental task of reverse-engineering a machine from scratch.

It was a monumental task but not an impossible one. Based on the clues garnered that night, pieced together with other tidbits that came their way, they produced a working model. The working model was called Red, perhaps as a tip of the hat to the codebook that had been photographed almost 15 years earlier. With it, ONI was again able to translate the Japanese naval codes to plaintext English. It was an absolute triumph. Never before had the security surrounding an electro-mechanical device designed for cryptology ever been breached. The experience led directly to the cracking of the Purple machine in 1940.

By 1937, the Japanese intelligence services had connected with their German counterparts. The Japanese had found it increasingly difficult to penetrate American secrets, owing in large measure to the physical dissimilarities between Asians and Caucasians. They looked to the Germans for help with infiltration. The Germans, for their part, were seeking intelligence on the Soviet Union. And Japan's assets, particularly its listening posts in the East, would fill a number of gaps there. It was a marriage of convenience.

At the same time, Japan stepped up its efforts in secure communications. Still unaware that the Americans were reading their dispatches, they nonetheless were taking no chances. One of the last transmissions decoded from Red, in February 1939, was the announcement that henceforth messages would be sent using a new system. The official Japanese designation of the machine was *97-shiki O-bun In-ji-ki* (Alphabetical Typewriter '97). The Americans, those few who knew about it, called it Purple.

It was not a simple thing. It consisted of two electric typewriters, each connected through a series of 26 cables, into a central black box. The cables would be unplugged and switched to different connections depending on the day. These, in turn, would feed current to a set of four rotors housed in the central box. The operator would switch cables and physically adjust the rotors to match that day's settings. All this switching and adjusting resulted in a truly astronomical number of potential settings. The plaintext message would be rendered into ciphertext and then superenciphered by the Purple machine prior to transmission.

It fell to two groups, the army's Signal Intelligence Service (SIS) and the navy's OP-20-G, a branch of ONI, to crack Purple. It was yet another daunting challenge.

They didn't have to start from scratch . . . not quite. For the better part of 20 years, the Americans had been reading secret Japanese messages, and some clues had been gleaned. They knew, for example, that diplomatic messages were formulaic. The openings typically said something along the lines of "I have the honor to inform Your Excellency." This was a clue for the new system.

Purple

During World War II, the Japanese based their Purple encoding machine on the Enigma machine used by their German allies. The cover has been raised in this photograph to show the encrypting rotor mechanism. (National Archives and Records Administration)

Then, too, since it was a new system, mistakes were made in transmission. Some messages would start their transmission in Purple but be relayed in Red. Like the Rosetta stone, real clues were provided here. Still, it wasn't quite enough. Those tasked with solving the puzzle were looking at the problem in terms of a refinement of the Red system. It hadn't yet occurred to them that Purple was an entirely new machine.

For nearly 18 months, late into the night and on weekends, the teams labored in vain. They'd awake in the middle of the night with an idea and rush to the office, only to find it went nowhere. They'd follow a promising lead, only to have it dead-end in gibberish. They were working themselves to death; indeed, one of the team leaders suffered a nervous breakdown in the process and was hospitalized for 6 months. With paper, pencil, graph paper, and slide rule, the analysts poked at the fringes until, painfully and slowly, patterns began to emerge.

Finally, a civilian technician working with the SIS team had an epiphany. Leo

Rosen realized that telephone switches would make the same type of combinations and connections as were beginning to appear. They attacked the Purple puzzle from this point of view, and within a month they had a plan on paper for an electrical device, using off-the-shelf telephone switching equipment. It was a machine that they believed would solve the problem.

Rosen built the beast at a cost of less than $700 and in less than a week. They called it the Purple Analog. And once again Americans were reading what the Japanese believed were their wholly secure communications.

It was a feat that was unlike any other in the annals of cryptology. Not only were the ciphers once again an open book but also it had been accomplished without ever once even getting a look at the Japanese machine. The Americans of SIS and OP-20-G had reverse-engineered a complex piece of equipment—complete with random rotor settings, electronic relays and switches, two sets of cables, and two typewriters—that none had ever seen. If it weren't for the gaunt faces and haunted eyes of the group, one might be tempted to think that they had pulled it out of thin air.

William Friedman, American genius and perhaps the greatest cryptologist who ever lived, was behind the program. He led the team that built the Purple Analog. Friedman began to call his people "magicians." The name stuck. In fact, the military would give the code name "magic" to all intelligence gained from interception of Japanese messages.

Magic began to flow in September 1940. But it would flow to a very few, select

Enigma logo

The original Enigma logotype, as it appeared on plates attached to the machines. (National Cryptologic Museum)

individuals. The president was on the list, of course, as were several cabinet members and the top military brass. But that was the limit. Any dissemination of "magic" beyond that level was to have been presented in such a way that it could have been derived from a number of sources.

While American eyes were focused on the Pacific, events of a similar nature were taking place in Europe.

In 1923, a small German concern produced a machine for encrypted communications that they called Enigma. It was initially designed for commercial communications, as a way of sending secure communications between offices for financial transactions, proprietary information, and the like.

The first model was large and cumbersome and had limited appeal. But the second model, introduced a year later, was much more compact, about the size of a portable typewriter. It caught the attention of the *Kriegsmarine* (the German navy). Tests were conducted, and Enigma was adopted and deployed for use at sea in 1926. The German army began to use it three years later, and the air force followed in 1935.

Enigma in the Field

The German Army's Enigma, deployed in the field. This image, captured after World War II, shows a typical installation. Three men were required to properly work the system. (National Archives and Records Administration)

Housed in a wooden box, the machine had a standard typewriter keyboard. The operator would type the message in plaintext. As he depressed each key, an electronic impulse would be sent through a series of rotors, which would scramble the signal. The rotors did not move in tandem, nor did they always move in uniform progression. It was in the variations of the steps between the rotor movements, coupled with the starting point of each rotor, that would provide what was thought to be an unbreakable cipher. The coded letter would light up on a panel at the top of the machine. The fully encoded message would then be transmitted. A three-man team was required for operation: one to read the initial message, one to type it into Enigma, and a third to read the lighted panel.

Modifications were made to the commercial model, to further enhance security. A fourth rotor was added to the original three, for example. And procedures for changing the positions of the rotors on a daily basis were developed. The Germans believed their system to be unbreakable. (The Japanese apparently agreed and borrowed the rotor concept, incorporating it into their Purple machine.)

The Germans, however, were unaware of the efforts of Poland's intelligence service to crack their communications. Poland was in a unique position, from both political and geographic viewpoints. After having finally gained independence following World War I, the Poles were concerned (and rightly so) that they would be prime targets of conquest by Germany on one side and the Soviet Union on the other. It was in Poland's vital national interest to keep track of what was happening just outside its borders.

Hitler came to power as chancellor of Germany in 1933, and adopted the title of führer a year later. Poland became increasingly concerned about the growth of Germany's military machine. Provocative statements demanding the return of territory taken from Germany at the end of World War I did little to ease tensions.

Poland's intelligence service had been reading German communications since 1926. And when Germany switched to Enigma, Poland acquired the commercial version of the machine.

Using their knowledge of Enigma technology, the Poles mounted an all-out attack on German communications. Initially they met with some success. But when Germany began its modifications to the commercially available Enigma, Poland was stymied, and by 1931 it was in the dark.

Help came from France. The French, and to a lesser extent the British, were also concerned about events taking place within Germany. And French intelligence had started their attempts to read the new German ciphers. They, in turn, received a boost from a German traitor, Hans-Thilo Schmidt. He was a walk-in who worked in German military communications. For a fee, he provided the French

with enough information to allow them to make substantial progress in cracking the advanced Enigma system. So by the end of 1932, France, Britain, and Poland were once again privy to German communications.

Germany continued its modifications to Enigma throughout the 1930s. With each twist, Poland was able to just barely keep pace. They finally built a machine, a rudimentary computer, actually, to automatically read German messages. This machine (dubbed "the Bombe" because it made ticking noises as it worked) ran a series of six modified Enigmas. By brute force it would run through a long series of rotor combinations until plaintext would begin to appear.

They finally got it working when the Germans added one more modification that increased the number of possible permutations tenfold. Poland's COMINT again went dark.

Great Britain and France entered into an agreement with Poland in 1939 to come to its aid in the event of an invasion by either Germany or the Soviet Union. As part of its contribution to the agreement, Poland agreed to share its Enigma technology with the two other partners. Modified Enigmas had been shipped to both France and Great Britain just weeks before Germany's blitzkrieg on Poland. When Germany then turned its eyes on France and overran the country in 1942, Great Britain was left holding the Enigma bag.

Britain's COMINT activities were centered in Bletchley Park, a large Victorian manor roughly 50 miles northwest of London. There a group of scholars, mathematicians, and linguists were recruited from Cambridge University to work on Enigma. A much more sophisticated version of Poland's Bombe was constructed, and even before France fell, the Allies were reading German military communications.

On America's entry into the war, intelligence services from the various Allied nations met to coordinate their activities, COMINT chief among them. The Canadians, the Australians, the British, and the Americans agreed to share assets (technologies, listening posts, and personnel) and divide responsibilities. The British learned of the Purple Analog; the Americans learned of the Enigma system. And a new code word was adopted. Intelligence gleaned from Enigma intercepts was to be termed *Ultra*.

Neither Germany nor Japan even suspected that their communications had been breached. Each successive modification to Enigma or to Purple brought fevered activity from Allied code breakers. And each was met, and overcome, in short order.

Magic and Ultra were to be two of the most potent weapons in the Allied arsenal throughout the war years. Intelligence gathered from these sources played decisive roles in all theaters of operations. It was through Ultra that Eisenhower knew the German Afrika Corps was unprepared for the landings in North Africa. It was through Magic that MacArthur learned the itinerary of Japanese Admiral Isoroku Yamamoto's flight across the South Pacific (intelligence that resulted in the downing of the plane and the death of the commander of all Japanese naval forces).

Successes in World War II COMINT were not limited to the Allies. The Germans had made remarkable strides themselves, including penetration of the private telephone conversations between British prime minister Winston Churchill and American president Franklin Roosevelt.

The two had developed a close working relationship long before America entered the war. Churchill realized that Great Britain would soon be isolated as more and more of the European continent fell before the German war machine, and he knew that he would need help from the United States if his country were to survive. For his part, Roosevelt was challenged by a large and vocal contingent of the population that wanted nothing to do with another war. The isolationists, led in part by Charles Lindbergh, were politically active and would tolerate no move that would bring the country closer to a war footing. Roosevelt knew that the United States would need Great Britain to remain defiant, if only to act as a buffer against Hitler.

So the relationship between the two elected leaders grew, fostered at least in part by numerous and frequent transatlantic radiotelephone conversations. They believed the conversations to be secure, since they were conducted using state-of-the-art scrambling equipment. The problem was that state-of-the-art at that point was nearly 20 years old. It was established, stable technology and was widespread, with transmitters and receivers around the globe. It involved splitting the radio band into specific frequencies and bouncing the signal (the human voice) between

frequencies during transmission. The signal would be run through a series of electronic filters during the process. The result would be just so much noise to anyone listening in without the appropriate equipment at the other end.

Modifications were made to the system in 1937 to increase security. The new system, called A-3, allowed for more than 3,800 possible combinations of frequencies and filter combinations. Not all of these were considered secure, and only six were actually used.

The Germans were listening. An interception station had been established in the Netherlands, and all radiotelephone conversations between the United States and Great Britain were monitored. The equipment installed there allowed for nearly instantaneous translation of the conversations overheard. And what they overheard was some pretty interesting stuff, particularly when Mr. Churchill and Mr. Roosevelt got to talking.

Both, of course, were master politicians. And both understood the value of direct contact. The opportunity to cut through diplomatic red tape was too good to resist. Firm in their belief that their communications were secure, both took full advantage of the technology, much to the pleasure of the Germans. They spoke not only with each other but also with their ambassadors and other world leaders, and they continued to do so until early in 1944, just months before the Normandy invasion. Full transcripts of the conversations were made and distributed by the German military intelligence services.

SIGSALY

In mid-1942, AT&T's Bell Laboratories received a contract to develop a new system for secure communications. They called it SIGSALY. Although it certainly sounds like an acronym, the initials in the name didn't stand for anything; it was just a name. The overall apparatus consisted of 40 racks of equipment—tubes, relays, and connectors—and weighed more than 50 tons. It incorporated two turntables for producing random noise. The entire machine required precise temperature control, identical at both transmission and receiving stations, and

CHURCHILL SPEAKS

When the SIGSALY system was perfected and about to be deployed in London and Washington, President Roosevelt had a concern.

Prime Minister Winston Churchill had a set of secret war rooms underground in the Whitehall section of London. With its reinforced ceilings and walls, it was where he would endure the nightly bombings of London by the German Luftwaffe. And it was here that he conducted much of his business during the war. He had living quarters within this enclave, and he was never far from his situation rooms, staff, or telephone.

Churchill was prone to making calls at all hours of the day or night. Roosevelt, however, was concerned that this new secure system would make it just a little too convenient for Churchill to pick up the phone and give him a call.

So while Churchill had his SIGSALY unit installed close to Whitehall, with a direct connection to the war rooms, Roosevelt opted to have his installed in the Pentagon, across the Potomac River in Virginia. Close, but not too close. He could still be reached in a real emergency, but it would be inconvenient for the lieutenant on duty to wake his commander-in-chief on a whim.

After all, sometimes there are better things to do at 3:00 AM than to enjoy a good friend's rhetoric.

Sir Winston Churchill. Prime Minister of Great Britain during World War II. (*National Archives and Records Administration*)

precise clockworks so that both sending and receiving stations would be absolutely synchronized. The system required 15 operators at each end.

It was the first system to employ pulse code modulation and was one of the earliest to use spread-spectrum technologies. Both technologies would be further developed after the war and would lead to the development of the digital audio, video, and data transmission systems used by present-day computers.

And it was secure. When it was deployed in late 1943, initially with stations in London and Washington, the German listening posts noted an immediate drop in A-3 traffic and concluded that another system was in place. They were never able to tap into SIGSALY. Eventually, stations were deployed around the world. Installations took place in North Africa, Australia, Hawaii, Guam, Paris and, following V-E Day, in Frankfurt and Berlin (West Berlin; the Soviets were never made privy to the system).

The complicated set of procedures and protocols, the manipulation of pulse codes, and the splitting of bandwidths and frequency spectrums opened an entirely new realm of technologies. These advances, coupled with the newfangled computing machines the army was developing, opened wide the doors to computer encryption systems.

THE RISE OF COMPUTER ENCRYPTION

The army started ENIAC (Electronic Numerical Integrator and Computer) with an initial contract in 1943. It needed a machine that could quickly and accurately calculate ballistics. What it got, when the machine started functioning in the fall of 1945, was a machine capable of rapid computations, along with the start of a revolution in information technology.

By the standards of the day, it was a marvel. This behemoth contained 30 distinct computing units, composed of more than 19,000 vacuum tubes, 1,500 relays, and thousands and thousands of resistors, capacitors, and inductors. It required forced-air cooling and weighed more than 30 tons. It was awesome in its ugliness, with its miles of exposed wires, blinking lights, and gauges. But it worked, and it could store up to 30 numbers at once. It was a good start.

Cray Supercomputer

State-of-the-art in the late 1970s, the Cray-1 supercomputer could store 1,000,000 words and perform 40,000,000 calculations per second. It was a long way from the World War II-era Bombe. The Soviet Union could not keep pace with the technology. (U.S. Department of Energy)

As computers grew in power and shrunk in size, they became standard equipment for cryptologists. In fact, much of the early development of mainframe computers in the 1950s and 1960s, the minicomputers of the 1970s and 1980s, and supercomputers of the 1990s was funded by the CIA and NSA.

DARPA (the Defense Advanced Research Projects Agency, formerly known as Advanced Research Projects Agency, or ARPA), an independent agency under

the Department of Defense, spearheaded much of the technology growth. DARPA was founded in the late 1950s as a reaction against the Soviet *Sputnik* satellite program. Never again, according to its mandate, would the United States be taken by surprise by the technological advances of another nation. It would oversee and fund advanced research into a wide range of emerging technologies. It was DARPA that pioneered direct connections and communications between remote computers so that in the event of a nuclear war, the nation's computing power would not be lost. When it started, this small network of computers, primarily based in large universities and government installations, was called ARPANET. As the network grew and more computers came online, it became the Internet.

ARPANET necessitated the development of new levels of electronic security. Without locks on the door, as it were, anyone with access to an online computer terminal could theoretically log on to any computer in the system and read the contents of the files contained there. Computer passwords were born.

As personal computers and inexpensive modems began to appear on desktops in the 1980s, the need for security increased exponentially. Everyone, it seemed, was starting to log on. And not just people within the United States; it was getting to be a World Wide Web of connected computers. Lots of information was flowing through central servers. And the programs required to intercept the flow were neither difficult to write nor to use. Potential threats came not just from foreign governments but also from the tech-savvy kid next door.

Computers communicate by sending packets of information across the network to a desired destination. Most of this is wholly transparent to the computer's operator. The packet contains details about where the information originated, where it is going, how the file should be reassembled on receipt, and a short piece of the information itself. Computer files are automatically segregated into these packets and sent on their way. The receiving computer automatically sends a message back confirming receipt of the packet and telling the sending computer that it is ready to receive the next packet.

Along the way, the packets are subject to interception by a third computer that just happens to be watching. If the people behind these watching computers are in the mood, they may try to open the files they intercept and read the contents. If the information has not been encrypted, the reading will pose no problem. If, on the other hand, the information has been encrypted, the watchers may be slowed down a bit.

Computer encryption, in theory, is little different from the encryption methods discussed earlier. It can consist of transposition or substitution ciphers, rendering a plaintext original into ciphertext. The difference is that with computers involved, the substitutions and/or transpositions become much more complicated and can be completed much quicker than, say, Thomas Jefferson ever imagined when he developed his wheel nearly 200 years ago. And the potential for superencryption and super-superencryption rises with the speed of the machine's components.

A number of commercial software applications exist that will provide for automatic encryption of files or e-mail. The problem, of course, is that these applications are widely available, and if you've got it, the chances are good that whoever wants to read your data will also be able to get it. So encryption alone is not the answer.

The next step is something called a digital signature. A digital signature is an added level of encryption, but one that is unique to each individual. When an operator logs on to his or her system, usually by entering a password at start-up, the system knows who is working the keyboard. (This is just one of the reasons to keep passwords secret. For added security, some next-generation systems allow biometric readings—fingerprints or even voice prints—for log-on.)

Assuming that appropriate software is installed on the sender's computer, each file is automatically encrypted with an algorithm unique to that user (an algorithm is a rigid set of procedures that take place one after another in a specific pattern to produce a desired outcome). Think of this process as a recipe: Do this, then add this, then put it in the oven for so long, and you wind up with a cake. The computer algorithms involved with digital signatures are the same idea. But each algorithm is slightly different from all the others, so everybody winds up with a slightly different cake. The cake in this example is the encryption.

It all gets complicated rather quickly, which is, of course, the general idea. Everything gets stepped up to another level: Simple messages are encrypted for

transmission over the Internet. Packets are created, and these, too, are encrypted. Digital signatures are added for yet another level of encryption. Special certificates are created that allow the receiver to ensure that the file with the digital signature really came from who it says it came from, and so on. And it is all done in the background, automatically and without any human intervention.

CHAPTER 5

Hide 'n' Seek

The Sea of Japan, 15.5 miles off the coast of North Korea, January 23, 1968.

I T HAD BEEN A CRISP AND COLD MORNING, BUT THE SKY WAS CLEAR for a change, and the ionospheric conditions that had been hampering operations were beginning to abate. It looked like the command would finally be able to begin its mission of gathering SIGINT (signal intelligence) and ELINT (electronic intelligence) on KORCOM (the North Korean Communists) communications. Up to that point, storms in the area and very little activity had combined to frustrate efforts to intercept much of anything in the way of transmissions. But just that morning the situation was beginning to change, and the technicians in the SOD Hut were picking up enough to give them hope.

SOD Hut was verbal shorthand for the Special Operations Detachment compartment aboard the ship. Before heading out on the mission some 10 days before, it had been crammed with electronic eavesdropping gear, recording devices, and cryptographic equipment, in addition to the charts and maps and documents and publications all bearing the purple- and red-ink stamp smudges that announced their "top secret" status. Thirty members of the ship's compliment of 84 were technicians assigned to the SOD Hut; it was they who would be spinning the dials and recording the intercepts for transmission, first to Japan and then on to Fort Meade, Maryland.

The mission was to patrol international waters, just outside the territorial limits on the east coast of North Korea, in an effort to intercept the electronic communications of the other side. Of particular interest on this trip were the methods employed by the Chinese, the Russians, and the North Koreans, particularly with one another.

It hadn't been going too well. Weather had plagued the mission from the start. The seas and the wind had been almost too much for the aging ship to punch through, and even some of the saltier members of the crew had gotten seasick. Superstructure and antennas were coated with ice, a blanket almost three inches

The United States Navy's environmental research ship, the *USS Pueblo*. Converted from a World War II-era cargo ship, it was deployed off the coast of North Korea in 1968 with a mission to gather ELINT (electronic intelligence). (National Archives and Records Administration)

thick. It wasn't quite a hazard to stability and navigation, but it wasn't far from it. The ship had arrived late on station. The stormy conditions had frustrated attempts to hear anything other than static and the moans of sick men.

So the clear weather and calm seas were viewed as good news. This was the first mission of the newly recommissioned USS *Pueblo,* and hopes were high. It was to be part shakedown cruise and part test of the concept of eavesdropping while in plain sight, with the emphasis on training and testing the largely inexperienced crew.

The ship had started its life during World War II as a cargo ship belonging to the U.S. Army. In 1966, she was transferred to the navy and given a new mission. Designated AGER-2 (Auxiliary General Environmental Research), the *Pueblo* was converted into a seagoing platform to perform ELINT operations. She became an element of Operation Clickbeetle, a joint program of the navy and the NSA. Her cover was that she was a vessel of scientific research, conducting oceanographic experiments and testing the waters for salinity and temperature, among other things.

It was a thin cover, to be sure, but at the time it was deemed adequate. The Soviet Union had itself been operating a similar program for years. Soviet fishing trawlers, bearing an unusually high number of antennas, had become a common sight to American sailors.

Crew of the USS Pueblo.

The crew of the USS Pueblo following their release by their KORCOM (North Korean Communist) captors. (National Archives and Records Administration)

The trawlers would somehow find themselves in the midst of a fleet exercise in the open ocean. Or they would sail just outside the territorial limits of the United States for years, paying a great deal of attention to the fishing grounds just outside the Portsmouth Naval Station in New Hampshire and Newport News in Virginia. When they would "accidentally" stray inside the American territorial limit, the U.S. Navy would inform them of their navigational error and escort them back to where they were supposed to be. In the Cold War, no shots were ever fired. No ships were boarded or detained. We kept an eye on them while they were keeping an eye on us.

The new AGER vessels would be lightly armed and would stay in international waters, posing no threat. And they would perform scientific research, carrying two oceanographers aboard.

"Remember the Pueblo" Button

The seizure of the USS Pueblo, and subsequent imprisonment of her officers and crew, by KORCOM (North Korean Communist) forces in 1968 sparked public outrage. This contemporary button harkened back to similar perceived outrages regarding the Alamo, the USS Maine, and Pearl Harbor. (Kismet Images)

Since the *Pueblo* was under orders to play by these rules, the risk assessment of the mission was officially "minimal." Commander Lloyd Bucher, captain of the ship, was told he could count on help from the U.S. 7th Fleet and the U.S. 5th Air Force based in Japan. But since the risk was minimal, no special support was requested from either command.

So it was that the crew was just sitting down to lunch, feeling better about the prospects for their mission. Perhaps if the *Pueblo* hadn't been under orders for radio silence or had been able to receive reports about earlier transgressions by the North Koreans, the crew might not have been quite so sanguine.

North Korea had violated the treaty that ended the Korean War by transgressing the DMZ (demilitarized zone—a no-man's-land that separated the north from the south) more than 50 times during 1967. For instance, in January 1967, a team of 31 North Korean soldiers, dressed in the uniforms of South Korea, had crossed the DMZ on a mission to assassinate the president of South Korea, with a secondary mission of destroying the American embassy in Seoul. They had gotten to within a city block of the presidential compound before they were discovered and stopped. All died in the attempt. The *Pueblo* was not told of this or other incidents.

So when Commander Bucher received a call in the wardroom telling him that a KORCOM vessel was eight miles out and approaching fast, he was not overly concerned. He had just verified his position as being some 15.5 miles offshore, roughly 1.5 miles into international waters. Besides, just the day before, two KORCOM fishing trawlers had approached and circled the *Pueblo*, coming within 25 yards before moving off. It was considered routine harassment.

Minutes after the first call came a second. The vessel was now fewer than five miles off and was approaching at full speed. Bucher went topside just in time to begin what was to become an international drama.

The vessel was a sub-chaser, fully armed, and the crew appeared to be at battle stations. It asked *Pueblo*'s nationality, and Bucher raised the Stars and Stripes in reply. The sub-chaser then signaled, "Heave to or I will fire." Bucher replied by signal, "I am in international waters." He *was* in international waters; he had just checked again and confirmed his position at 15.8 miles from the nearest shore (12 miles is the international limit).

By this time, the sub-chaser had been joined by four KORCOM torpedo boats. They began to circle *Pueblo,* and their fully armed soldiers were making preparations to board. Bucher ordered *Pueblo* about, so as to present a smaller target and to begin to move farther out to sea.

The sub-chaser opened fire with her 57-millimeter guns while the torpedo boats racked the superstructure with machine-gun fire. Four members of the crew, including Bucher, were wounded.

In the SOD Hut, crew and technicians alike were attempting to destroy as much of the classified equipment and documents as was possible. Bucher stalled for time. He had received a message telling him help was on the way in the form of aircraft from Japan.

- -

The sub-chaser now signaled that *Pueblo* was to follow her to Wonson. *Pueblo* started slowly moving toward shore. When the ship was well inside the territorial limit, she was stopped and boarded, and the crew was taken prisoner.

U.S. insistence that the ship and crew be returned was met with North Korean insistence that they had captured spies well within their territory. The ship was impounded; the crew became prisoners of war of the Democratic Republic of North Korea.

Treatment of the crew was brutal. They were beaten for minor, or nonexistent, infractions of the rules. Medical treatment was withheld. They were fed a diet of turnips and water. In addition to the physical punishments, they were required to participate in propaganda broadcasts and were forced to admit they were the transgressors. During "free" news conferences, attended by members of the press from Communist nations, the crew spoke of the good treatment they were receiving and hinted that they might wish to defect to North Korea.

GETTING IT PAST THE CENSORS

That's what they said, but that's not what they were *really* saying. Forced to confess to spying on the peaceful people of North Korea, they named Maxwell Smart (a character of a popular television situation comedy) as their case officer.

One confession stated, "We as conscientious human beings who were cast upon the rocks and shoals of immorality by the tidal waves of Washington's naughty policies know that neither the frequency nor the distances of these transgressions into the territorial waters of this sovereign peace-loving nation matter, because the penetration however slight is sufficient to complete the act." According to Bucher's account of the incident, "rocks and shoals" refers to the military uniform code of justice, while that last phrase is a definition of rape.

In one photograph, designed to show the crew rested and relaxed and in perfectly good health, the term *snow job* is displayed in American sign language by members of the crew.

The crew had instituted a version of steganography, designed to get the real

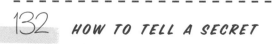

message past the censors. The North Koreans believed their persuasions and punishments and threats of even worse treatment were making an impression on their prisoners of war (POWs), getting them to admit to all sorts of nefarious activities. An impression was indeed being made, but not the one the KORCOMs had envisioned. Anyone in the West who was paying attention was receiving the real message.

At first these attempts at clandestine communications were tentative, since the crew was concerned about what would happen if they were discovered. But when the first efforts slipped through undetected, the system was employed with greater frequency and dexterity.

In one photographic session, Commander Bucher himself stood and saluted the

The Hawaiian Good Luck Sign

Members of the crew of the *USS Pueblo* flash the Hawaiian good luck sign for their North Korean Communist (KORCOM) captors. The derisive nature of the sign was described by *Time* magazine. (Corbis)

camera with a single, upraised middle finger. There was no retribution; apparently the KORCOMs were unfamiliar with the gesture.

The idea for the signal came from newsreels that the captors used to entertain the crew. The crew members would regularly be herded into a hall to view movies. Usually the films depicted glorious and heroic feats accomplished by North Korean soldiers or athletes. One such movie night contained two short films, both newsreels. The first showed the North Korean soccer team visiting London. On the streets, they were greeted at one point by a British businessman, complete with bowler and umbrella, offering the middle-finger salute to the team. The second showed the return of an American serviceman killed in action. As the remains

PIG LATIN

ourFay orescay andway evensay earsyay agoway ourway athersfay oughtbray orthfay, onway isthay ontinentcay, away ewnay ationnay, onceivedcay inway ibertylay, andway edicatedday otay ethay opositionpray atthay allway enmay areway eatedcray equalway

Pig Latin is the name given to a method of jumbling the language, usually the spoken language, in such a way that the meaning is both clear and distorted at the same time.

The idea is to take the first part of the word and put it at the end and adding *ay* or *-way*. If the word begins with a consonant, or multiple consonants, they are moved, leaving a vowel sound at the beginning of the word; an *ay* is then tacked on. If the word begins with a vowel, the first syllable is moved and *way* is added.

Thus . . .

how	becomes	owhay
to	becomes	otay
tell	becomes	elltay

were given to United Nations personnel, a U.S. naval officer on the scene also offered the one-finger salute.

The upraised middle finger soon began to appear in North Korean propaganda photographs and films of the crew. Sometimes a sailor would use his middle finger to push back eyeglasses as a camera panned past, to scratch a nose, or to rest a head against. Sometimes it would be used in group shots.

As the KORCOMs were unfamiliar with the gesture and it began to appear with some frequency, they began to question it. Universally, the gesture came to be known as the "Hawaiian good luck sign." The jailers were told the sign was native to the islands of Hawaii, and it was a wish for good luck and prosperity. As such, it was allowed to continue to appear in photographs of the crew sent across the world in news photographs.

```
a         becomes      away
secret    becomes      ecretsay
```

There are a few other rules and exceptions, but if you've got this part, you've pretty much got it.

It takes some practice to get it right, both in the sending and in the receiving. And it can be done only if both sender and receiver are fluent in English. It would be too confusing for one who isn't well versed in the language.

As the passage at the top suggests, the meaning becomes somewhat obscured but not so much so that it becomes difficult to discern the true meaning. As with any skill, the more pig Latin is practiced, the easier the translation becomes.

There is anecdotal evidence to suggest that it was used widely among prisoners of war (POWs), particularly in World War II. Many of the guards had a rudimentary command of English but not enough to penetrate the mysteries of pig Latin. But the steganography wasn't good (all those *ay* sounds were a bit suspicious), so it had to be employed with discretion.

Then, at the end of October some six months after it was initiated, use of the sign came to a sudden halt. *Time* magazine blew the cover story on October 18, 1968. It printed one of the photographs and revealed the gesture's true meaning. And it triggered a period of the most severe treatment as yet sustained by the crew.

Finally, on December 23, 1968, 11 months to the day following their capture, the crew was repatriated. They came home as heroes to the public and the press, but not necessarily to the navy.

Quite a bit of classified material had fallen into KORCOM hands. The United States had suffered a black eye. It was believed, by those in command at the time, that not enough had been done to secure the secrets and that members of the crew, particularly Commander Bucher, had violated the Uniform Code by providing propaganda to the enemy. He had cooperated, it was said.

Commander Bucher faced an official court of inquiry when he returned home. A panel of five admirals recommended his general court-martial for surrendering the ship to search and seizure, but the secretary of the navy declined, saying he "had suffered enough." Bucher died in January 2004, in part from complications of the beatings he suffered while in captivity.

The surviving crew members were awarded Prisoner of War Medals, by special act of Congress, in 1989. They were ineligible until that time because officially they were detainees rather than prisoners, since the United States hadn't been at war with North Korea at the time of the incident.

The USS *Pueblo* itself remains on the active rolls of commissioned ships of the U.S. Navy. It is anchored in Pyongyang, the capital of North Korea. She has been transformed into a museum and is a popular tourist attraction in the north.

The crew of the *Pueblo* understood the two essential ingredients of steganographic communication: steganography and communication. In other words, if they wanted to communicate their disdain for the propaganda they were forced to create, they knew they had to hide the message. They had to find ways of getting the message past the KORCOM censors. If their captors had intercepted and understood the message before it went out, no communication would have taken place. Worse, as the crew learned the hard way, there is usually a stiff penalty to be paid when the communication is found out.

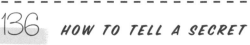

CENSORSHIP IN WARTIME

Velvalee Dickinson learned that lesson the hard way too when she was fined $10,000 and sentenced to five years in a federal prison for violating wartime censorship laws. It could have been much worse for her, since she was actually passing intelligence to the Japanese during the height of World War II. She did it with steganographic communication through the mails.

Mrs. Dickinson owned and operated a doll shop in Manhattan. From her Madison Avenue address, she sold and shipped rare and antique dolls around the country and, before the start of the war, around the world.

Among her prewar contacts was Ichiro Yokoyama, a Japanese naval attaché in Washington, D.C. Together they developed a working code based on the doll industry. A certain kind of doll, designated by country of manufacture, would stand for a class of warship. Using this code, Mrs. Dickinson would pass information she gathered on to Japanese intelligence. Or at least that was what she thought she was doing.

Actually, her letters weren't getting through. She'd type letters that sounded like personal, chatty notes, full of news of the children, her garden, and her doll collection, and then send them off to a friend in Buenos Aries, Argentina. The problem was that her correspondent in Argentina moved and left no forwarding address. So the letters came back. But they didn't come back to Mrs. Dickinson, because she didn't use her name or address on the return envelope. She used, instead, the names and addresses of doll-shop customers who lived in Springfield, Ohio, or Colorado Springs, Colorado, or Spokane, Washington. The customers became suspicious when they received the returned letters, and they turned them over to the FBI.

At least 10 letters were forwarded to the FBI. And it was apparent that something wasn't quite right. The FBI labs were able to determine quickly that although the letters were composed on different typewriters, they all had a common author. The punctuation, spelling errors, and sentence structures all matched.

An examination of the content proved unsettling. One of the letters spoke of Mr. Shaw, who had been ill but was now fully recovered and would be back to work soon. That was a little too close to the mark, since the USS *Shaw*, a destroyer severely damaged during the attack on Pearl Harbor, had been repaired and was on its way to rejoin the Pacific fleet.

Visits to the purported letter-writers revealed they all had one thing in common: a certain New York doll shop. The FBI paid a visit to Mrs. Dickinson and caught up with her while she was at her bank, with an open safe-deposit box containing some $13,000 in marked bills. The serial numbers on the bills had been recorded earlier, before the war, so it was a simple matter to trace them from Mrs. Dickinson's vault straight back to the Japanese embassy.

The censors were able to catch what was happening only because the letters drew attention to themselves by being just a little out of the ordinary. Multiple letters, from multiple people, mailed at random times from a variety of cities, was actually a pretty good system. If the contact in Buenos Aires hadn't moved or had left a forwarding address, the letters never would have come to the attention of the FBI and the steganography would have worked.

Counting on you

This World War II-era morale poster for the American home front was a reminder that any information regarding the war effort was potentially valuable to the enemy. (U.S. Air Force)

The role of censor has never been an easy one. Traditionally Americans are very protective of their right to free speech and expression. The Founding Fathers were well aware of this and incorporated these freedoms into the Constitution's Bill of Rights, giving them primacy as the First Amendment. Attempts to abridge these rights, beginning with the Alien and Sedition Acts of 1798, have met with scorn and opposition, and battles over them continue to make their way to the Supreme Court in the twenty-first century.

Still, particularly in times of war, the government has imposed strict rules of censorship. While most governments have long histories of strict limitations on what can be sent through the mail and other forms of public communication (newspapers, radio, and magazines), particularly during times of war, the United States adopted systematic censorship of both civilian and military communications only during World War II.

In the hours immediately following the attack on Pearl Harbor, great debate centered on the amount of information that was to be made public. Censorship policies were not yet developed or in place. While some government officials argued for telling the whole truth regarding the extent of the damage done, others, primarily in the military, argued for releasing as little information as possible. The more restrictive approach won.

On the night of December 9, 1941—two days after the attack and one day after the formal declaration of war on Japan— President Roosevelt took to the airwaves for one of his "fireside chats." Reportedly more Americans listened to that broadcast than any other program in radio history to that point. His words were carefully guarded. He said the losses suffered during the attack were serious but that he hadn't yet received the reports that would allow him to "state the exact damage." In fact, the White House and the Pentagon knew exactly what had happened by that point but made the determination not to share the details with the public.

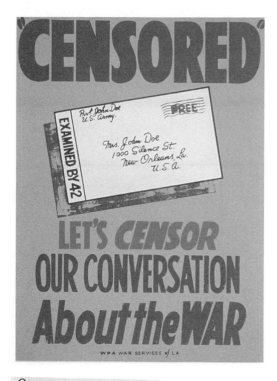

Censored

This World War II-era morale poster for the American home front was a reminder that any information regarding the war effort was potentially valuable to the enemy. (Library of Congress)

The navy in particular was concerned about disseminating information that would give aid and comfort to the enemy. The information that flowed from that source was little and usually incorrect. Regarding the aftermath of Pearl Harbor, in

"LOUIE, LOUIE"

The song "Louie, Louie" was written in 1955 by Los Angeles musician and session player Richard Berry. He wrote it as a love song, from the point of view of a young man telling his bartender (Louie) about a trip he was about to make to see his girl. It had Jamaican-styled lyrics and a calypso beat. His recorded version had some minor success on the R&B charts before passing into obscurity.

Other bands in other cities recorded the song, none meeting with anything other than regional acceptance. And not much was heard from the song after that until the Kingsmen picked it up in 1963 and put to tape their famous version of the song.

The Kingsmen was a garage band with a small following, playing in and around Portland, Oregon; they had an opportunity for a gig on a cruise ship, and they needed a demo to get the job.

So they booked a recording session at a studio in Portland (at a rate of $36 an hour). A single dangling boom microphone was placed above vocalist Jack Ely. It was set purposely high, to catch less of the vocal sound and more of the instrumentation. The producer of the session, Ken Chase, didn't like what he was hearing on that first take, so he raised the microphone even

"Louie, Louie." The original 45-rpm single, on Jerden Records, of "Louie, Louie," recorded by the Kingsmen. (*Kismet Images*)

higher to get even less of the unpleasant sound. So on the second take, Ely attempted to mimic a Jamaican accent while standing on tiptoe, head back, and shouting at a microphone above his head. The band went a little more up-tempo and the beat was more rock 'n' roll than calypso. It was this second take that was released as a single.

The single version of the song became a hit and reached number 2 on *Billboard*'s Hot 100 chart. Like many hits of the day, it started to fade quickly after it reached its peak. That probably would have been the end of it if the State of Indiana hadn't gotten involved.

The governor, Matthew Welsh, had received reports that the lyrics included profanity and that the Kingsmen had deliberately slurred the words so they'd be harder to detect. It was "common knowledge" that

The Kingsmen. From left: Mike Mitchell, Barry Curtis, Dick Peterson, Lynn Easton, and Norm Sundholm. *(Courtesy of Dick Peterson)*

when the 45-rpm record was actually played at 33 1/3 rpm, the real meaning could be discerned. On the basis of this, the governor banned airplay of "Louie, Louie" within the state.

News of the events in Indiana had two results: First, the alleged lyrics came to the attention of Attorney General Bobby Kennedy, who requested that the Federal Bureau of Investigation (FBI) undertake a thorough investigation (an investigation personally directed by an

(cont.)

(cont.)

outraged J. Edgar Hoover), and, second, it pushed sales of the single through the roof.

For more than two years, the laboratories, scientists, and officers of the FBI worked on the case. The band was interviewed. Record company executives were interviewed. Multiple copies of the record were obtained, from various parts of the country, and put through a series of tests. The records were played at the correct speed; they were played at slower speeds; they were played at faster speeds. FBI officers attended live concerts trying to understand what the band was singing.

Finally, when it finished its investigation some 31 months later, the FBI issued its report: The lyrics weren't obscene; they were simply unintelligible.

particular, the navy was far less than transparent, hinting that the bulk of the Pacific fleet was already at sea, undertaking offensive operations by seeking out the enemy. In fact, the bulk of the Pacific fleet was resting on the bottom of Pearl Harbor. As ships that had been damaged or sunk were brought back into service, only reluctantly did the navy let information become known. Months later, when one such ship rejoined the fleet, a journalist started his story, "Seven of the two ships sunk at Pearl Harbor have now rejoined the fleet."

Private civilian communications also experienced a level of impromptu censorship during wartime. The job of monitoring international mail, telephone calls, and telegrams fell to the army. Yet the first censors did not arrive at local post offices until the week following the attack. The reasons for this were simple: first, there weren't enough trained personnel available from the peacetime army, and second, there was no system in place. Local post offices were not under centralized control from Washington. Each answered to the governors of their states. There simply was no efficient way to maintain such constant monitoring.

However, once a system was cobbled together, it worked well. All international mail was opened and read. Likewise, international cables and telegrams were reviewed prior to dispatch. International telephone calls were subject to taps and monitoring. The censors became skilled at their trade, and a number of clandestine channels of communication between spies and their controls were closed. Several private codes, such as Mrs. Dickinson's dolls and a similar one using flowers, were exposed, and those involved were soon investigated by the FBI.

Censorship of military personnel was particularly rigorous. All letters, all packages, and all postcards were subject to inspection, regardless of destination. The folks at home grew accustomed to receiving letters where words or entire passages were blacked out or literally cut out. Undoubtedly there were attempts at steganography buried in missives to loved ones, parents, or friends. But officials undertook a serious campaign to dissuade such attempts, and the penalties, if any attempts were discovered, were severe.

Yank, a popular weekly general-interest magazine for the military, reported regularly on the efforts of the military censors with admonitions to their readership to be very careful in what they wrote. As an illustration, in 1944, they reported on one beleaguered censor who discovered two letters from a soldier in a single batch of mail. One was addressed to the soldier's wife, the other to his girlfriend. To his wife, he complained that she was spending too much money on frivolities (movies and entertainments and steaks). To his girlfriend, he included a promise of dinner and a show on his next three-day pass. The censor noted, with interest, that the soldier had inadvertently put the letters in the wrong envelopes. Since the censor's job was to monitor the military content of the mails and not personal content, he placed the letters back into the envelopes from which they came and sent them on their way. Some secrets will come out if the sender isn't careful.

Wartime censorship was not limited to the news and private communications. Publishing houses and the film industry were also under scrutiny. Teams of censors were based in New York City to review books due to be released, in Los Angeles to screen movies, and in Rochester, New York, to look at the home movies processed there. It wasn't moral content or literary merit that was judged; rather, it was the references to military operations, to attitudes toward Allied nations and issues that might impact civilian morale that received attention.

It was a short step from wartime necessity to peacetime good intentions that shifted the focus of censorship following the collapse of the Axis powers. The Federal Communications Commission (FCC) assumed the mantle of protector of the nation's morals when it came to the broadcast spectrum. First with radio, and later with television, the FCC imposed rules of decency and decorum. The Post Office Department was charged with the task of policing the materials that were distributed through the mail.

CAMOUFLAGE AND DISGUISE

Truly effective camouflage draws no attention to itself. The idea is not necessarily to hide an object from view but to present that object as not being there in the first

Camouflage

This squad of World War I-era doughboys is in camouflage. The leaves and twigs break the natural shapes of helmets. (Kismet Images)

place. By breaking up regular outlines and forms, or by matching color and texture of the surroundings, the object blends into the surrounding area.

If watchful eyes are looking for a soldier in the woods, consciously or unconsciously, those eyes will seek outlines and forms that are not associated with the stuff of the woods. Those eyes, in combination with the brain, will attempt to place items in context, and focus on elements that do not fit the particular context. Straight lines (rifles) or regularly curved objects (helmets) are not to be found in nature; they are out of context. Human-made constructs call attention to themselves, and the eye will be drawn to investigate. However, if these regular forms are obscured, the eyes will continue to scan, passing over the camouflage.

The objective of camouflage, therefore, is not to hide the object but to have the object blend into its surroundings. Tactics change with circumstances. A soldier in jungle camouflage, uniform, and paint simply isn't going to blend into the background during a snowstorm.

HUNTER'S CAMOUFLAGE

Many sportsmen believe their specialized camouflage gives them an added advantage over their game in the wild. The newest designs in the outdoor shops feature earth tones of browns and greens and blacks and patterns complete with leaves, branches, and moss. It would certainly appear, at first blush, that these togs would allow hunters to conceal themselves in the deep woods. And while walking through the tall grass with these items on, it is easy to see how that idea would be reinforced.

What many hunters fail to realize, however, are the fundamental differences between animals and people. One of these differences is that most animals are color-blind. Whether humans wear hunter green or fluorescent orange really makes no difference to a deer. Another difference is that most animals have a far keener sense of smell than do humans. What this means is that to be successful, hunters needs to camouflage not their clothing but their scent.

MONTY'S DOUBLE

Field Marshal Sir Bernard Law Montgomery (known as "Monty") commanded the British 8th Army during World War II. As the principal field commander for the British, his activities were of great interest to his Italian and German enemies, and his movements were closely monitored. It was hoped that he would give a clue as to where the Allies would strike next.

Allied planners working on Operation Fortitude (the campaign of misdirection designed to keep the location of the D-Day landings a secret) decided to make use of Monty's fame in their operations. It was decided to send a body double on a

Monty. British Field Marshal Sir Bernard Law Montgomery. *(National Archives and Records Administration)*

tour of Mediterranean military installations, the theory being that Montgomery would never be away from headquarters if the invasion was imminent. It was hoped that appearances by Montgomery would lead the Germans to believe that the invasion was still sometime in the future.

Meyrick Edward Clifton-James had been a professional actor before the war and had volunteered for the British Army with the intention of entertaining the troops. The army believed, however, that he would be much more useful in other ways, so as a commissioned Lieutenant he was assigned to the paymaster's corps.

While working in Leicester his resemblance to Montgomery was noted, and news of it was passed up the chain of command.

About three months before the D-Day landings, he received a phone call from Colonel David Niven (Niven too was an actor; he served in MI5, the British spy service, during the war). Clifton-James was summoned to London to take part in a film being produced. On his arrival, he was briefed on Operation Copperhead. Clifton-James was to portray Montgomery on the Mediterranean tour.

Monty's double. M.E. Clifton-James, a British actor before World War II, assumed the role of double for Field Marshal Montgomery during the weeks leading up to D-Day as part of Operation Fortitude. *(National Archives and Records Administration)*

Clifton-James joined Montgomery's staff for a period of roughly two months, with a mission to study the field marshal. He was to mimic Monty's physical movements, his patterns of speech, and his posture. Then, at the end of May 1944, only two weeks before the invasion, Clifton-James began the tour.

The first stop was Gibraltar. From there he moved on to several stops in North Africa, and finally to Egypt where he went into seclusion until the Normandy landings were well established.

It didn't work too well. Montgomery was a nonsmoking teetotaler. Clifton-James was a heavy smoker with a drinking problem. He would reportedly show up drunk and reeking of tobacco. Not a lot of people were fooled.

Following the invasion, Clifton-James went back to his paymaster's position. But following the war, he wrote a best seller, *I Was Monty's Double* (his version had a different interpretation and a slightly different ending). In 1958 he starred in the movie version of the story.

The plain brown wrapper approach to sending materials through the mail worked at first, since it was designed to blend into the background with all other packaging. It worked, that is, until the plain brown wrapper was used more frequently and became more noticeable, defeating the whole purpose.

Although related, disguise is an entirely different discipline from camouflage. Disguise is the art of changing the appearance of an object or person to give the impression that it is something, or someone, else entirely. When disguise is employed, there is the assumption that the object will be seen by watching eyes. The mission of disguise is to have the watching eyes see, but not recognize, the object or person.

Disguise is much more than just changing outward appearances, however, particularly when referring to a person. Yes, facial features can be altered by placing cotton in the cheeks (as did Marlon Brando when shooting *The Godfather*), adding glasses (*Superman*), growing or removing facial hair (Paul McCartney grew a mustache in 1967 while recording *Sgt. Pepper's Lonely Hearts Club Band* to hide a scar received in a motorcycle accident), changing a hairline (Leonard Nimoy playing Mr. Spock) or changing scars, teeth, or the structure of the nose with prosthetics. An essential element of the plot of *Dr. No* has James Bond surgically altered to appear Japanese.

At least as important are the intangibles that go into a character. This is where acting comes into play. Everything about the person must change, but in such a way as to be natural and to call no attention to itself.

Disguise of inanimate objects is also possible. This is truly the realm of spies, with hollowed-out boot heels and coat buttons that are actually microphones. Again, the assumption is that the object will indeed be seen. The objective is to have it pass through the censor's hands without careful investigation.

MIS-X

During World War II a supersecret operation, run by MIS-X (a very small detachment of the U.S. 8th Army Air Corps), sent information and material to American prisoners of war held by Germany in POW camps. So secret was this operation that it was known only by its post office box number, 1142. But so successful was 1142 that it was able to ship material and receive information from at least 64 German POW camps.

Fort Hunt, Virginia, was home to 1142. Located along the banks of the Potomac River, just 10 miles south of Washington, D.C., and next to George Washington's Mount Vernon home, Fort Hunt itself was a classified military installation. Locals thought it was a processing center for German POWs, a transit camp where prisoners would be processed before moving on to permanent camps elsewhere in the country.

It was that, but it was much more. It was also a center for interrogation of German prisoners. The tactics employed did not necessarily conform to the letter of the Geneva Conventions. For example, listening devices were placed in prisoners' cells to catch conversations. And true prisoners would be joined by U.S. military personnel, disguised as prisoners, to help guide conversations. All this was illegal and, of course, top secret. The existence of these activities was not made public until well after the war.

But even this was a cover. For within the fort, and off limits to just about everyone, were a few select buildings. Within those walls, clandestine war was being waged on "the barbed-wire front," as the prison camps came to be colloquially known.

MIS-X had created three humanitarian aid organizations. These organizations would ship packages to the U.S. prisoners in Germany. The packages contained toiletries, decks of cards, games, and other items that, it was hoped, would make the prisoners' lives just a little easier. That's certainly what it looked like they were sending.

However, cribbage boards were actually radios. Anything with a handle (hairbrushes, for example) contained reichsmarks and compasses. Game boards were hollowed out and filled with maps and forged documents. Decks of cards, when treated with water, would reveal pieces of maps. These pieces, when put together like a jigsaw puzzle, would show the major roads and waterways of Europe. Guns, ammunition, saws, knives, and more were smuggled into the camps. All manner of material that might be useful to escaped prisoners was smuggled into the camps.

The prisoners called their theater of operations "the barbed-wire front." They knew that although they were captured, they were not out of the war. Their new mission was to distract the enemy while they plotted their escapes.

EASTER EGGS

There are secrets lurking in your home. They come from outside sources—computer operating systems and programs, DVDs, audio CDs, and quite possibly the TV show you watched last night. They are called Easter eggs, and they are everywhere.

Technically, an Easter egg is an undocumented feature that has been purposely added to otherwise overt content. The definition is stretched a bit when it includes inside jokes incorporated into broadcast television shows. True Easter eggs are harmless and are usually of a whimsical nature.

In the early 1980s, when personal computers were just coming onto the market, software publishers were concerned about the ability of hackers to copy what they considered to be their intellectual property (that is, the core code of their programs). It was fairly easy to get at the core code of a program, and the laws against it weren't all that clear at the time. So little undocumented subroutines were added before applications were released. This way, if the core code was stolen and adapted for another application, the undocumented feature would also be incorporated into the new program. And that would constitute proof of the theft.

But it appears the practice really took off later in the 1980s when programmers were not always

It worked. Not only did these materials get past the censors who were opening and inspecting the parcels, but information was also flowing out of the camps. The radios were transmitters and receivers. The prisoners could receive information and instructions, and they could report back with lists of who was there, who was safe, and who was not.

With the surrender of Germany and the liberation of the POW camps, 1142

given official credit for their work. To show they were involved, they'd bury a little something in the code, just to prove they were there at the start. Sometimes a special set of credits would appear when you punched a certain set of keys in sequence. Sometimes it was more elaborate, as in Microsoft's Excel 1997, where a flight simulator was embedded (the mouse would be used as the controller).

Whatever the origin, the practice has become epidemic. Easter eggs can be found in virtually all versions of computer operating systems (UNIX, Linux, Windows, and Macintosh), in many popular software programs, in computer games, and even in some hardware configurations (certain printers and scanners will play "Ode to Joy" if you turn them on the right way). You can find them on DVDs, both in the movies and the special features. Some audio CDs have them in the form of unlisted bonus tracks. They've also been found in cell phones, Mr. Coffee machines, and in programmable Whirlpool ovens. Television shows sometimes incorporate them as running gags (the number 47, for example, appeared in most *Star Trek* episodes).

The practice isn't condoned officially. Nevertheless, literally thousands of Easter eggs have been documented, and more appear with every software or DVD release. Several Web sites, such as http://eeggs.com and http://www.eggheaven2000.com, attempt to keep pace with developments.

was dismantled . . . with prejudice (an euphemism from covert operations, meaning "to kill"). All records and documents relating to the program were burned. The buildings themselves were leveled, and the ground paved over. The intention was that program was never to be known. So complete was the destruction, and so quickly was it implemented, that by the time of the Korean War, less than three years later, all operational knowledge and expertise was lost. Only scattered and incomplete references to the program still exist.

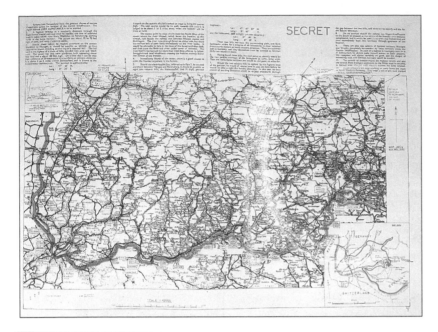

MIS-X map

During World War II, the supersecret American operation MIS-X would distribute materials and supplies to captured airmen and soldiers through parcels shipped to German stalags by charitable organizations. Concealed within a deck of otherwise ordinary playing cards, for example, was an escape map, showing prisoners of war the route to freedom. The map would be cut into 52 equal pieces, with one hidden in each card. When the card was soaked in water, the face would separate from the backing, revealing the piece. The individual pieces would then be reassembled, like a jigsaw puzzle, to form the complete map. (Courtesy of American Playing Card Company)

MICRODOTS AND MISDIRECTION

While all this was going on in Virginia, the Germans were developing technology of their own. One of the more interesting pieces that survived well into the Cold War was the microdot. J. Edgar Hoover, director of the FBI and the man tasked with domestic counterintelligence operations, called them "the enemy's masterpiece of espionage."

The microdot is the product of a three-stage photographic technique. First the document to be transmitted is photographed conventionally and printed at the size of a postage stamp. This is then photographed again, this time using a special microlens on the camera. The resulting image on film is less than 0.05 inch in diameter. Once the film has been developed, it is transferred using a hypodermic needle. The resulting negative is roughly the size of the period at the end of this sentence. Something that small can be placed just about anywhere . . . including in a book or a newspaper or a letter. It can then be sent, via mail, anywhere in the world.

The FBI first heard about this technology shortly before the outbreak of World War II. Correspondence from suspected spies was then combed for samples. One was finally found in 1942 when a lab technician noticed a glint from one area of the letter he was examining. It was light reflecting off the film.

After the war, the Soviet intelligence services adopted and refined the technology, eliminating the reflective properties of the film and producing a more compact apparatus for producing the microdot.

Techniques for transmitting the film improved as well. The dots would be placed beneath the postage stamp on the outside of the envelope. Or slipped into the binding of general-interest magazines, which would then be wrapped and sent on their way. Use of the microdot continued through the mid-1960s.

Yet another technique for slipping past watchful eyes is misdirection. One of the reasons it works so well is the acknowledgment that someone is indeed watching. The idea is to give the watchers something to see over here, while the really important activity is happening over there.

Consider the events of mid-June 2006 as a case in point. President George W. Bush was at Camp David in the hills of Maryland, roughly 90 miles north of Washington, D.C. With him were members of his cabinet, members of the National Security Council, assorted aides, and department heads. The stated purpose of this two-day working retreat in the woods was to formulate and coordinate "next steps" with regard to diplomatic and military actions in response to the latest developments in the war in Iraq. A series of in-depth sessions had been outlined

CARRIER PIGEONS

The use of photography to reduce the size of the message to be transmitted was pioneered by the French during the Franco-Prussian War (1870-1871).

It was during that war that the city of Paris was completely surrounded and cut off from all outside communications. The Prussians who had laid siege to the city had cut all telegraph lines and weren't about to let the mail go through. Parisians had tried a number of avenues to pass communications past the Prussians, including floating watertight balls containing missives down the Seine and sending messages aloft in balloons, but none proved effective.

Enter L'Esperance, the pigeon-racing club of Paris. They suggested strapping messages to the tail feathers of the birds. For it to work, however, the messages would have to be small and lightweight. The solution was to produce photographic copies of the original messages. These would be printed on paper roughly 1.5 inches square and rolled into a tube. The tube was strapped to the pigeon, and off it went. During the eight months of the siege, nearly 60 messages got past the watchful eyes, and guns, of the Prussians.

Parisian soldiers on horseback carrying pigeons. *(Kismet Images)*

weeks in advance, and video conferences had been scheduled to take place during the day on Monday and Tuesday.

Perhaps no one in the world is watched as closely as the president of the United States. The Secret Service knows where he is at all times (gone are those heady days of giving his guards the slip). Logs are kept of his visitors, along with the length and nature of his meetings. Often a photographic record is made. And telephone logs are meticulous in their detail. Wherever he goes, whoever he sees, and whatever he says is news. And representatives of all media outlets follow in his wake.

George W. Bush was known to go to bed early, usually by 10:00. So it was no surprise when he excused himself from the Monday-evening gathering saying that he was turning in for the night. Several of the day's participants were heading back to Washington that night aboard the marine helicopter that brought the president to Camp David; it was time for them to depart. So the notebooks were closed and the cameras were shut down for the night. The misdirection had worked.

While most of the people who were usually watching turned away, the president started moving. The secret was that it was the president, not staffers, on the helicopter. Rather than returning to the White House, it touched down at Andrews Air Force Base. Across the tarmac was *Air Force One*, and barely 10 minutes after the helicopter landed, President Bush was once again in the air. He was headed to Baghdad.

When the White House press corps gathered for their briefing on Tuesday morning, they were shown live television pictures of their president half a world away and meeting with the new leaders of Iraq. All eyes had been turned to Camp David for the anticipated second day of meetings while the real news was taking place somewhere else entirely.

Misdirection becomes much more difficult in an era of high-tech gadgetry and blooming video surveillance. Because of the attacks of 9/11 in the United States and the growing number of terrorist attacks around the world, local and national governments have invested heavily in placing cameras in public spaces to monitor goings-on. In the United Kingdom, for example, more than 1.5 million cameras have been installed in public spaces since the beginning of the twenty-first century, although exact numbers are not available. It has been estimated that the average Londoner is on camera no less than 300 times a day.

PASSWORDS

Magician and escape artist Harry Houdini would astound audiences with his ability to escape from just about any trap into which he was placed. Audiences loved it when he was placed inside an airtight safe and given just 10 minutes to break out. Houdini was fond of the trick too because he knew that it was a lot easier to break out of a safe than it was to break into one. All the security was on the outside. Once he was in, he was all set.

So it is with many computer systems. Once you're in, you can find your way around fairly easily if you know what you're doing and where you want to go. The hard part is getting in. And as it turns out, that isn't nearly as hard as it sounds.

Computer security firms report that nearly half of all survey respondents know at least one other person's password. What makes this even more troubling is another fact: nearly two thirds of computer users use the same password for both personal and business computers.

People who choose their own passwords tend to pick just one and stick with it, using it repeatedly on different Web sites, both secure and nonsecure. And they tend to pick something that can be easily remembered (mother's birth name, birth date, child's name). Or they will choose a simple and memorable six-letter combination, such as a word that can be found in a dictionary.

The problem with this is that there are programs out there designed to detect passwords, and they will crunch through thousands of combinations in a second in seeking a match. Most of the programs begin by going through dictionaries (and not just English dictionaries, so if you think you're being security-minded by using Latin or Czech . . . forget it).

Other popular choices are the names of pets, sports teams, or fictional characters from popular culture. There is also the popular expedient of using the number 1 in place of a lower-case *L*, or *0* rather than *O*.

The reason all this is danger-ous is that hackers will not nec-essarily target an individual when attacking a company's com-puter system. Rather, they will run their program on the entire system, and the chances are good that out of 1,500 people, some-one's mother's birth name was *Ri-vera* or someone else is a fan of Mr. Spock.

People also tend to make a note of their passwords. Some-times they are kept "safe" in a wallet or purse. Other times they are put on a sticky note and "hidden" under the keyboard. Or maybe the sticky note is just placed on the monitor itself.

In May 2006, a British firm un-dertook a study to learn the most common passwords. The results:

#10	*Thomas*	(0.99% of all respondents)
#9	*Arsenal*	(1.11% of all respondents)
#8	*monkey*	(1.33% of all respondents)
#7	*Charlie*	(1.39% of all respondents)
#6	*qwerty*	(1.41% of all respondents)
#5	*123456*	(1.63% of all respondents)
#4	*letmein*	(1.76% of all respondents)
#3	*Liverpool*	(1.82% of all respondents)
#2	*password*	(3.780% of all respondents)
#1	*123*	(3.784% of all respondents)

A similar survey undertaken in the United States would probably produce similar results. (Al-though *Liverpool* and *Arsenal*, two of the most popular British foot-ball teams, wouldn't make the list, chances are that *Cowboys* and *Yankees* might.)

God, sex, and *money* are popular passwords. One site that catered to the young and single crowd re-ported a predominance of *stud, goddess,* and *cutiepie. Secret* is very popular, as is *Terces* (spell it backward).

Many organizations have been

(cont.)

(cont.)

security-conscious regarding passwords (the Department of Defense has a 30-page guideline for password security procedures) and have requirements that they be changed regularly. And people will adhere to these strict guidelines, for about two weeks. Then they will go back to their old ways and their old passwords. That's exactly what the hackers are counting on.

So here are the rules:

1. *Change your password frequently.* It should be done every two weeks, or every three at the most.
2. *Use a combination of letters and numbers.* Don't use common words or names.
3. *Don't use the password for more than one purpose.* If you use it for e-mail, don't use it for a system log-on or to protect files.
4. *Don't share your password with anyone.* Period.
5. *Don't write it down.* Anywhere.
6. *Change your password on Monday morning.* If you use it during the day and for the balance of the week, you will find it easier to remember than if you change it right before you go home on Friday afternoon.
7. *Try to follow the rules for longer than two weeks.*

At the same time, advances in technology related to digital photography have finally changed the rules of the game. The first rule to go is "Pictures don't lie," and the second is "What you see is what you get." Neither is necessarily the case any longer.

FUN WITH PIXELS

When a digital camera, or scanner, captures an image, it does not do so by looking at the entire scene. Rather it breaks the scene into a grid, like a checkerboard.

Each tiny square, called a *pixel* (short for "picture element"), is assigned a color. The number of pixels in the grid determines the amount of detail captured. The detail captured is referred to as resolution. The greater the number of pixels, the greater the detail captured and the higher the resolution. Traditional television screens display images at a resolution of 52 pixels per inch. Computer monitors display images at 72 pixels per inch. Computer printers generally require at least 300 pixels per inch (less than that, and the pictures start to look fuzzy; square blocks of color become visible, and the picture is referred to as "pixilated"). Commercial printing presses do best with even higher resolutions, in the 600 pixels per inch range.

The resolution refers to the number of pixels in a vertical direction.

But recall that, like a checkerboard, pixels are stacked both horizontally and vertically. So, if you set your monitor to display images at 1024×768 (a common setting), you are instructing the computer to display 1,024 pixels horizontally by 764 pixels vertically.

Each pixel is analyzed, and a color is assigned. The colors of the real world are converted into three distinct layers: red, green, and blue. This is the red-green-blue (RGB) spectrum that lives inside computers. For most contemporary computer applications, 8 bits of information are recorded for each color, producing a 24-bit color image (8×3=24). It is the varying intensities of red, green, and blue that combine to produce the millions of colors that appear on the screen or printed page. An image of a park, for example, would have high intensities of green and much less red and blue, whereas an image of the sky on a sunny day will have greater intensities of blue and lesser intensities of green and red.

But even if you were to take an image of the top of a pool table, looking straight down and seeing nothing but the green felt, the camera would still record information in the blue and red bits. The information may be that there is nothing there, but it is still recorded.

All this information, 24 bits per pixel multiplied by the total number of pixels, produces large individual files. Files of 20 megabytes are common; in the world of commercial graphics, a 60-megabyte file is considered adequate. It is in these large files that other information may be embedded.

LEONARDO DA VINCI'S REAL SECRET?

Leonardo da Vinci's *Mona Lisa* is one of the most recognizable images in the Western world. For centuries, kings and common folk, scholars and the uninitiated alike, have been in awe of the piece. It is a marvel of perspective and of technique. It shows a depth and a harmony that has only rarely been achieved. It is truly the work of a master operating at the very peak of his powers.

It has been studied. It has been analyzed. Its pigments have been tested. Its history has been probed and documented and traced.

Leonardo's Real Secret? When scientists superimposed Leonardo da Vinci's self-portrait over the *Mona Lisa*, they were surprised to discover that the facial features bore a striking resemblance to one another. Was the *Mona Lisa* another self-portrait of Leonardo da Vinci?

(Courtesy of Dr. Lillian Schwartz)

Entire careers have been built around this one piece of art.

But there is at least one question that will never be answered with certainty: Is the lady laughing with us or laughing at us? What is she smiling about? Are we missing something? Is there an inside joke here?

According to Dr. Lillian Schwartz, an artist and a pioneer of computer imaging, the *Mona Lisa* may not be what she at first appears to be. Schwartz developed her theory while working with other scientists at Bell Laboratories. The *Mona Lisa* was the subject for another project altogether. It was during the course of the work that Schwartz superimposed a known self-portrait of da Vinci, executed during his later years, on the *Mona Lisa*. No one expected to find what suddenly appeared self-evident: Everything matched.

Using the nose as a guide, the two images were made precisely the same size. When the two were brought together, it was clear (to those proposing the theory, at least) that they were looking at the same face. The positioning and depth of the eyes on one exactly matched the other. So did the width of the forehead and the facial structure and musculature. The conclusion was obvious: the *Mona Lisa* was da Vinci's self-portrait.

Schwartz does not stand alone in her conviction. At the same time, there is more than a little controversy here, and many art historians remain skeptical.

Leonardo da Vinci is generally regarded as one of the most brilliant minds to have walked the planet. He was the master of many disciplines. There is no reason to believe that steganographic communications wasn't one of them.

So if Dr. Schwartz is correct, she may have uncovered Leonardo da Vinci's real coded message.

Computer programmers will tell you that it is not difficult to write a program to display images using only 7 bits of information per color channel, per pixel. The colors may not be quite as sharp and crisp, but to the uninitiated eye, very little difference would be seen. By displaying only 7 bits per color per pixel, quite a bit of room is left over (3 bits per pixel, to be exact). Those remaining bits in each pixel can be used for other data—a character, for example. And with a high-resolution file, the ability to embed quite a few characters exists. String together just a few characters and you've got a word; a few more and you've got a sentence; not that many more and you've got a secret message.

But the information embedded need not be character sets. This is an RGB file, after all. If each of those bits were used to record a color value, an entire photograph could be embedded. So while the file opens to display one image—a doll, for example—if 7 bits of information are stripped away, an entirely different image—a ship, for example—would appear.

The principle holds true not just for still digital photography but also for digital video and audio files. To the computer, it is all just a bit stream, a string of 1's and 0's. It is the computer's program that sorts it all out. So the MP3 file that the local garage band just posted on a public Web site may contain more than just their latest song. From that public Web site, anyone with a computer anywhere in the world can download it. With the right program, someone could reveal the song's hidden information.

The vulnerability in this scenario is the physical security of the Web site's computers. The hard drives containing all those files are subject to search and, possibly, seizure by the law enforcement agencies of the country where they reside. If the FBI can convince a court that there are illegal activities taking place on the site, it can obtain permission to physically remove the computers involved. And that could cause a disruption in the flow of information.

DATA HAVENS

One way to avoid the censors is to create a "data haven"—a safe location free from government agencies and law enforcement. An interesting example of a data haven is the Principality of Sealand. Sealand is a small island in the North Sea, roughly seven nautical miles from the Thames Estuary of England. It is just outside the territorial waters of the United Kingdom and, theoretically at least, not subject to the laws of any country.

It was built during World War II as an element in the United Kingdom's coastal defenses. It served as a platform for anti-aircraft guns and as a fort defending approaches to the Thames. The platform is constructed on two huge, hollow concrete pillars, with rooms inside the pillars for living space. Designed to withstand the ravages of the elements, the human-made island supported a garrison of 200 soldiers during the war. After the war it was abandoned, and it remained so for more than 20 years. But in 1967, a British entrepreneur, Roy Bates, moved his family to the island and took possession. Since it was in international waters, he claimed sovereignty. Roy Bates claimed the title of prince and declared that henceforth, he would be known as Roy of Sealand.

In 1968, and repeatedly during the following years, the United Kingdom has attempted to reassert its authority. But Sealand's struggle for freedom (as Bates called it) has received aid from the British courts. On several occasions the courts have ruled that since Sealand is outside the territorial waters of the United Kingdom, the courts have no authority to adjudicate.

Although Sealand has never been granted formal recognition as a sovereign entity, it is a true data haven. The rules are few and include prohibitions against child pornography and corporate hacking. Entities (corporations or individuals) may rent space on the computers and conduct whatever business they choose, free from government regulations or interference.

In early 2000, the economy of Sealand was given a boost when a privately held corporation moved its operations there, installing sophisticated computer equipment and high-speed data transmission links. The links have redundancies built in. By cable they extend in two directions: to the United Kingdom and to Continental Europe. As a fail-safe, in case either of those cable links is compromised or shut down, high-speed satellite links have been established.

As an added measure of security, the computers are housed below sea level, in one of the concrete pillars. In order to enter these rooms where the computers are housed, one must wear scuba diving gear because the rooms have been flooded with nitrogen gas. But to do that, one must first access Sealand. The only approaches are by air and by sea; both are closely watched. Any unauthorized approach will be—and has been—met with armed resistance.

Getting a message past the censors may be best accomplished by a data haven, where the censors are avoided altogether.

CHAPTER 6

National Secrets

New York City, July 1, 1893

THE UNITED STATES WAS IN THE MIDST OF AN ECONOMIC DEPRES-
sion brought on by the monetary policies adopted by the previous administration in Washington, D.C. It needed stability and it needed a strong
leader to put an end to inflation and bring the jobs back.

With those needs in mind, the country elected Stephen Grover Cleveland as the
twenty-fourth president of the United States (he had also been the twenty-second
president; he was the first and only president to serve nonconsecutive terms). Cleveland was to deliver a major address and set of initiatives to Congress in August.

But there was a problem. Cleveland had become aware of a rough spot on the
roof of his mouth. He didn't think too much of it, but he didn't want to ignore it either. He asked a friend, Dr. Robert O'Reilly, to take a look. The doctor discovered
a lesion, "nearly the size of a quarter with cauliflower granulation," according to his
notes. The president had cancer and required immediate surgery.

It wasn't quite that simple. The August address to Congress had been set and
announced; it could not be postponed without the probability of serious damage to
the cause. Further, the country needed to know that it was in the hands of a healthy
man (which it wasn't).

On what was billed as a vacation trip, the president traveled first to New York City, then on to Cape Cod for two weeks' rest and relaxation. While in New York, he boarded a friend's yacht, was met by a team of surgeons, and underwent the surgical procedure in secret.

Using a special clamp to draw back his cheek, the surgeons removed two teeth, most of his upper left jaw, and about half of the roof of his mouth. The tumor had grown to nearly the size of a golf ball. Once it had been removed, the cavity was packed with gauze. The vacation was used to allow Cleveland to recuperate. On his return trip, a vulcanized rubber prosthesis was fitted. The president wore this when he returned to the White House.

Since the surgery produced no external scars and the prosthesis worked so well, Grover Cleveland showed no visible effects of the operation. There was no swelling, bruising, or scarring. His face looked no different, and his speech returned without incident. He was able to keep his appointment before Congress. The Sherman Silver Purchase Act was repealed. The public never knew.

It wasn't until 1917, nearly 25 years after the fact and 10 years after Cleveland's death, that the secret was made known through an article in the *Saturday Evening Post* that had been authored by the chief surgeon with the family's permission.

SECRETS OF PRESIDENTIAL HEALTH

It wasn't the first time, or the last, that the president's physical condition was to be kept secret from the public. The cloak of secrecy surrounding a president's health was a tradition that stretched back to the days of George Washington.

Even in his day, Washington was presented as a large, strong, and healthy man. The truth was a little different. As a teenager Washington contracted rickets, which left him with a sunken torso. Most of his clothing was padded to hide the effects, and his shoulders were not quite as broad as they appeared. While still a teenager he contracted smallpox on a trip to Barbados, which left his face and body pock-marked. His hearing and eyesight began to fail during his presidency. And his full head of hair, once fiery red, was already a thing of history when he served. He was actually very nearly bald, and what was left of his hair was pure white during much of his tenure. And the last of his few remaining teeth had been pulled shortly after his first inaugural.

Gilbert Stuart had actually taken quite a bit of artistic license when he pictured Washington. Stuart left out the pockmarks, he fleshed out his cheeks, gave him a healthy pink skin (Washington actually had a rather pallid complexion), and put him in a full wig. That's how the country remembers Washington; that's how he is pictured on the $1 bill. In many ways, Washington was a giant and was exactly what the country needed at that point. Physically, however, he was just about as shaky as was the country. But the public good would not have been served if this had been general knowledge. And since there weren't any television cameras around at the time, the public didn't need to know.

Nor did it need to know, four score and seven years later, about Abraham

Lincoln. His bout with smallpox, contracted shortly after his famous speech at Gettysburg, was never reported by the contemporary newspapers. The country needed him to be strong during the Civil War.

After the assassination of James Garfield in 1881, Chester Arthur became the twenty-first president of the United States. Garfield was wildly popular, and his protracted death scene (he lingered nearly six months after he was shot) had taken a toll on the country. But the country needed stability after Garfield's death; it needed a robust and energetic leader. So when Arthur was diagnosed with "Bright's disease" shortly after taking office, it was decided to keep it quiet. The disease was a catch-all term for a variety of maladies leading to kidney failure. It was known to be a death sentence. Those who had it suffered growing fatigue as poisons circulated through the blood. When the *New York Herald* published the story, it was vehemently denied, with the White House stating instead that the president had a cold. The story died, and Arthur finished his term plagued by bad kidneys and heart problems. It was the combination of the two that finally did kill him a year after he left office.

Woodrow Wilson had suffered at least two strokes (unreported) before being elected president. But it was during his second term, shortly after the end of World War I, that he suffered a third. He was essentially incapacitated, and it was a secret from everyone. No one was allowed to see him other than his doctors and his wife. The vice president and the cabinet were kept at arm's length from October 1919 until the end of his term more than a year later. Even Wilson's chief of staff was kept in the dark.

The notion that the president's health was a national secret continued through the twentieth century. The country knew, in a vague way, that Franklin Roosevelt had polio, but it wasn't stressed. Virtually every photograph of him was taken from the waist up; almost none exist of him in a wheelchair. At the onset of his campaign for the presidency in 1932, he wore leg braces and would appear standing, supported by the arm of his son or an aide until he reached a podium, where he would support himself. The extent of his paralysis was kept hidden. Hidden, too, was his severe hypertension and heart condition. It was present during his first campaign and worsened during his tenure. Doctors discouraged him from running for his fourth term in 1944, but it was the height of World War II, and he

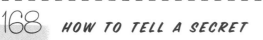

would not be dissuaded. Saying that he could not be distracted from the war effort during the campaign, he sent his vice-presidential nominee, Harry Truman, out on the stump. The country didn't know what White House insiders knew: Roosevelt would never survive a fourth term. On paper, the election was between Roosevelt and Thomas E. Dewey. The secret was that the choice was really between Dewey and Truman.

President Franklin D. Roosevelt

A rare photograph of Roosevelt in the wheelchair of his own design. (Corbis)

Presidential health secrets didn't end there. Eisenhower had suffered a massive (and unreported) heart attack before being elected president. Kennedy suffered from (again unreported) Addison's disease (a deficiency of the adrenal glands). Rather than to his actual (and often debilitating) condition, Kennedy's back pain was attributed to wounds suffered during World War II. His special rocking chair was pointed to with a degree of pride and misdirection; his crutches were almost never reported and were less frequently photographed. Also unreported was the cortisone and a concoction of painkillers that were kept stashed in bank safety-deposit boxes around the country (so they'd be handy while the president was on the road).

Famously, Lyndon Johnson showed the world the scar he received from his gallbladder operation. But he never showed the scar he received from the operation that removed the skin cancer from his ankle. *Cancer*, it was believed, was much too frightening a word to present to the public. Richard Nixon's phlebitis, potentially lethal, was not reported until he left office. And the public never knew how close Ronald Reagan was to death following the attempt on his life; instead the media fed the public news about the jokes the president told to his surgeons. In fact, it was an exploding bullet (that didn't explode) that lodged itself next to Reagan's heart. He had also suffered a collapsed lung in the attempt. Reagan's initial surgery for colon cancer was widely reported; the follow-up was not. Nor was the procedure to remove a skin cancer from his nose.

A TRADITION OF SECRETS

The keeping, and telling, of national secrets is traditional in America. George Washington was the country's first spymaster. He is reported to have personally run a number of assets during the American Revolution. One of his first acts after having taken command of Continental forces in 1775 was the expenditure of funds ($333.00, to be precise) to establish a network of spies in Boston to keep an eye on British military activities.

Approximately 10 years earlier, a group had been formed in Boston to protest and actively resist the Stamp Act, a British tax imposed on everything from paper to tea. These were the self-proclaimed Sons of Liberty. Their mission was to thwart the collection of the taxes by all possible means (legal and illegal) and to foment discontent wherever possible. The Boston group made contact with similar groups in Baltimore, Philadelphia, and eventually in each of the 13 colonies, and this, in turn, led to the formation of the Committees of Correspondence.

The Committees of Correspondence would trade news and information of activities under way to undermine British authority. They were the closest thing America had at the time to a unifying political force. Couriers with dispatches would be sent on horseback or by ship between cities in an effort to coordinate activities and organize resistance.

In Boston, it appears that the four principal members were Samuel Adams, John Hancock, Dr. Benjamin Church, and Dr. Joseph Warren. They assumed leadership roles in the earliest stages of the Revolution.

As a leader of the Sons of Liberty, a member of the Committees of Correspondence, and allegedly a participant in the Boston Tea Party, Dr. Church was a guiding force. Among those to whom he gave guidance was British General Thomas Gage, governor of Massachusetts and commanding general of British forces in North America. Dr. Church was a spy, and had been one since at least 1772.

It was Church who provided information to the British about the military stores being gathered in Concord, Massachusetts. He supplied details as to the whereabouts and quantities of the supplies on hand. Later, when the Colonies began to get organized, Washington had named him surgeon general of the Continental Army. In this position he became intimately familiar with the state of the army and its plans. He did his best to ensure that the British were as well informed as he.

It was only after one of his reports, written in cipher, was intercepted that Church's secret identity was revealed. Confronted by General Washington, Church offered dubious explanations. He was court-martialed as a spy and convicted. But at that point, Congress had not yet authorized the hanging of spies. So Church was sentenced to life imprisonment in solitary confinement. This was later changed to exile, and Church was sent to the West Indies. The ship carrying him was never heard from again and it is presumed that it and Church were lost at sea.

SPIES OF THE REVOLUTION

Perhaps one of the most successful operations on the American side was the Culper ring. Operating out of New York City and under the direct control of Washington, the ring provided intelligence on British forces and intentions. It was so secret that even Washington did not know the names of all the operatives.

At the center was Robert Townsend, a prominent New York merchant with well-known Tory leanings. As a principal supplier to the British Army then occupying Manhattan, he developed relationships with a number of officers. These contacts, in addition to his business dealings, provided him with a significant amount of valuable information. Using invisible ink (a formulation supplied by Washington), Townsend would write his reports and send them to his contact on Long Island. He would sign his reports with an alias (also supposedly supplied by Washington), Samuel Culper Jr.

Townsend employed added steganography by writing his reports on plain sheets of paper. These would then be slipped between other sheets, the whole package bundled together and shipped as one item among many, under the guise of a delivery, to his contact on Long Island.

The Long Island contact was Abraham Woodhull, a farmer living on the northern shore. Woodhull would add his report to Townsend's, again using invisible ink but signing them as Samuel Culper Sr., and send the entire package to Washington's headquarters.

Following Washington's explicit instructions, the Culper ring used dead drops, secret writing, aliases, and steganography to carry out its mission. Secrecy prevailed; Washington never learned the real identities of either Culper Sr. or Culper Jr. In fact, Townsend's role wasn't established until handwriting analysis revealed the secret in 1939.

SECRETS OF THE NEW NATION

In the early days of the Republic, the United States did not have a formal agency or organization for collecting or analyzing intelligence. Still, it was a recognized need, and Congress would appropriate funds to be used at the president's discretion. It became known as the Contingent Fund for Foreign Intercourse. Each president was required to give an accounting to Congress on its use, but an exception was made for "such expenditures as he may think inadvisable to specify." As early as 1790, therefore, the need for intelligence was codified, and under the direct control of the chief executive.

Virtually all the presidents availed themselves of this fund, usually employing confidential correspondents overseas on matters regarding commerce and treaties.

The correspondents would report to the president or in some cases to the secretary of state, through unofficial channels, of attitudes within foreign (primarily European) capitals toward proposed initiatives. Military intelligence was not part of the mission. It would be left to commanders in the field to use, or ignore, whatever intelligence came their way. This would be the case up through the Civil War.

Political intelligence was flowing in all directions during the opening administrations. Great Britain, France, and Spain all had interests in North America. None were too concerned about America's military machinery, which was all but nonexistent. But all were anticipating a collapse from within. Establishing such a large democracy had never been accomplished, and European powers believed this new union would soon disintegrate into regional factions. All wanted accurate and timely information regarding the expected demise of this new upstart.

Great Britain reestablished its information network among Tories immediately after the cessation of hostilities. Operating out of Quebec, George Beckwith, a lieutenant colonel in the British Army, traveled extensively, and openly, throughout the upper United States. Beckwith had commanded the British secret services during the Revolution after the execution of Major John Andre (Benedict Arnold's contact during the ill-fated attempt to surrender the fortifications at West Point on the Hudson River) and was well acquainted with the old network. He was also well known himself, and it was generally assumed that during his travels he was at least an unofficial representative of the Crown.

On one such trip he was approached by the new secretary of the treasury with a proposal to reopen commerce between the United States and British possessions in the West Indies. Alexander Hamilton wasn't a spy, but he was a member of Washington's cabinet. And in meeting with Great Britain's acknowledged representative, he at the very least provided insight into the political discussions and debates of the administration. Gaining this insight, of course, was Beckwith's mission. He would be hard pressed to find a better source than the secretary of the treasury. Hamilton was an avowed Anglophile and Francophobe and he advocated stronger ties with Great Britain, particularly after the horrors of the French Revolution became known.

To suggest that Hamilton was anything other than a patriot would be wrong. Still, he did serve as a conduit of information, so it can be correctly said that the

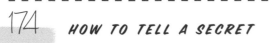

Edmund Randolph

Secretary of state in the cabinet of President George Washington, Randolph resigned under a cloud when evidence of his activities as a spy for the French came to light. (National Archives and Records Administration)

British had penetrated Washington's cabinet. Exactly how much, or how little, information he conveyed is a matter of speculation.

France, too, was seeking information, and apparently it had access through Edmund Randolph, Washington's secretary of state from 1794 to 1795. The details are sketchy, but it appears that Randolph offered to sell information to France detailing British involvement in the Whiskey Rebellion. Although it was never proved, Randolph was put in the uncomfortable position of having to face President Washington to answer the suspicions (charges were never leveled). After the incident, Randolph resigned.

General James Wilkinson, commander of the American Army from 1800 through 1812, was a spy for the Spanish. He had been on the Spanish payroll, with an annual

General James Wilkinson

A schemer and a rogue, he was the ranking officer of the American Army under Presidents Adams and Jefferson—and a spy for the Spanish during his entire tenure. (National Archives and Records Administration)

stipend of $2,000, since 1787. Generally regarded today as an absolutely amoral scoundrel and rogue, Wilkinson did everything within his power to advance the Spanish position in North America, including attempts to separate Kentucky and Tennessee from the Union. He had risen to his position through a covert campaign of political backstabbing and whispered libel that forced the removal of his superior officer, General "Mad Anthony" Wayne. During the War of 1812, he attained the rank of major general but accomplished little (at least he did no major harm). He finally retired from service in 1816 and went to Mexico, where he died and was buried in 1821.

With the exception of the Randolph affair, most of these activities would be undiscovered until long after the participants had died, and then such goings-on would be reported only with the posthumous publication of memoirs or diaries.

Just as the United States had no agency or organization charged with collecting intelligence, it had no agency or organization charged with counterintelligence. Indeed, the United States had nothing approaching a national police force, like the FBI, until 1908.

CIVIL WAR INTELLIGENCE

Americans have tended to view spying as something inherently dishonorable. It was somehow unsportsmanlike or deceitful. One's honor was considered to be a sacred thing, and a slur against it was taken as an insult with grave consequences. (Often, the consequences resulted in a duel, with the very real possibility of death to one or both of the participants.)

Professional intelligence officers did start to get involved during the Civil War, but the effort was haphazard and certainly far from uniform or national. Battlefield commanders were still responsible for their own tactical intelligence. Some would employ the services of independent scouts to keep abreast of the enemy's movements, although most used cavalry commands. Some would use their signal service or provost guard.

The closest thing to a national police force was a private organization run by Allan Pinkerton from offices in Chicago.

Pinkerton's detective agency was employed primarily by railroads before and after the Civil War. It was through these business contacts that he first came to know Abraham Lincoln, an attorney for the Illinois Central Railroad (Pinkerton had that contract) and George McClellan, president of the Ohio and Mississippi Railroad (Pinkerton had that contract, too).

When Lincoln appointed McClellan to command the Army of the Potomac, McClellan contacted Pinkerton and arranged for him to begin providing intelligence services. Pinkerton, in his postwar book *Spy of the Rebellion*, styled this as the start of the United States Secret Service, but that was significantly overstating the case. Pinkerton's loyalty seemed to have been more to McClellan rather than to the army or even the country. While he did catch some Confederate spies and ran operations in Virginia, even penetrating the Confederate secret service, he reported

Pinkerton & McClellan

Allan Pinkerton (left), self-proclaimed head of the United States Secret Service, worked closely with General George McClellan (right). Pinkerton provided the Army with widely exaggerated estimates of the strength of Confederate forces. This illustration originally appeared in the first edition of *Spy of the Rebellion*, Pinkerton's postwar account of his service during the war. (Kismet Images)

back to McClellan. At one point, he even spied on Lincoln, his cabinet, and the war department, feeding reports to McClellan. When McClellan was finally dismissed by Lincoln following the battle of Antietam, Pinkerton took his detectives and went home, too.

The next to lay a claim to the start of the United States Secret Service was Lafayette C. Baker. In his postwar memoirs, *History of the United States Secret Service,* Baker claims to have organized a national bureau for both intelligence and counterintelligence. Again, he overstated the position. Where Pinkerton was McClellan's man, Baker was General Winfield Scott's man. Baker did run some operations and was instrumental in tracking down John Wilkes Booth, but his organization was more akin to a police force than anything else. In fact, Baker and Pinkerton overlapped operations in Washington, D.C. for a short period. Whether the cause

Pinkerton Being Arrested by Baker's Men

Allan Pinkerton (barefoot, at left), self-proclaimed head of the United States Secret Service, is arrested by soldiers under the command of Lafayette C. Baker, another self-proclaimed head of the Secret Service. This illustration originally appeared in the first edition of *Spy of the Rebellion*, Pinkerton's postwar account of his service during the war. (Kismet Images)

was secrecy or divergent lines of communication is unclear, but both organizations managed to arrest officers of the other (Pinkerton himself was once taken into custody).

Even Lincoln had his own covert informant. William A. Lloyd was a publisher of railroad and steamer guides used throughout the South. At the start of the war, Lloyd asked Lincoln for a pass through Union lines so he could continue his business. Lincoln gave him the pass, but with the request that Lloyd report back to the president on conditions and attitudes in the Confederacy. He did, sending his reports to his wife's family in Maryland, who would then hand-deliver the packets to the White House. Lincoln presumably used the reports to check the veracity of what he was receiving from his generals.

The Confederate States of America wasn't much better organized in the realm of intelligence, although a network running from north to east Virginia and into southern Maryland allowed for a regular flow of mail, newspapers, and reports to the southern capital in Richmond. The network worked for most of the war, and in fact, Booth tried to use the network for his escape following the assassination. By that point, however, following Lee's surrender at Appomattox, the network had dissolved and there was little sympathy for Booth's actions. The support he was counting on never materialized.

Any expertise or institutional knowledge in the field of intelligence or counterintelligence that had been gained during the war was essentially lost with the peace. Operatives retired from military service and went back to their civilian occupations; provost marshals left federal service for police work in the cities. And no effort was made to retain an active secret service.

During the Civil War, the American military was the most powerful in the world. Both the army and the navy had been expanded to unprecedented levels. But following the war, rapid demobilization wreaked havoc on the military infrastructure.

The army had essentially two missions. The first was to police the South during the period of Reconstruction. The second was to protect citizens moving west, into and across the Indian territories. Neither required a huge standing military force.

The navy, an organization that revolutionized warfare during the Civil War with the introduction of ironclad warships, fell into a general state of disrepair. The number of ships on active duty plummeted; the number that was actually seaworthy was far lower. At the same time, the lessons learned during the American tragedy had not been lost on other nations, and their navies were updated and continued to grow.

DEVELOPMENT OF INTELLIGENCE SERVICES

It was only in the latter part of the nineteenth century, during the administration of Chester A. Arthur in the 1880s, that the federal government began to rebuild the navy. One of the first actions of his secretary of the navy, William Hunt, was to establish an Office of Naval Intelligence (ONI) within the Bureau of Navigation.

The term *intelligence* was not used in a way that General Washington might have recognized, nor does it mean what it has come to mean in the twenty-first century. Its mission, as defined at the time, was to supply ". . . the most accurate information as to the progress of naval science, and the condition and resources of foreign navies." The army's Military Intelligence Division (MID) was organized during the same period, but by the time of the Spanish-American War in 1898, it consisted of just 18 officers and enlisted men. These men, working out of the war department in Washington, would coordinate the efforts and reports of military attachés posted in a variety of embassies around the world.

Both ONI and MID were operating, independently, at the time of the Spanish-American War, and both made contributions, albeit small, to that effort. As had been the case after cessation of hostilities in all wars, rapid demobilization took place, and the functions associated with intelligence were again decimated. Both ONI and MID were downsized considerably, and their missions were limited to little other than obtaining maps of potential danger areas.

It wasn't until the onset of World War I that the army started to get serious and systematic about its intelligence. General John "Black Jack" Pershing assumed command of the American Expeditionary Force and reorganized the chain of command, following the model employed by the French Army. Under this new model, the occupation of intelligence agent (designated G-2) became a recognized and formalized staff function.

As the war was nearing its conclusion, the White House undertook an initiative that was to have far-reaching consequences. President Wilson was determined to win the peace as well as the war, and he was determined to form an international organization to arbitrate disputes among nations. The existing structure consisted of overlapping treaties and assurances of mutual defense between individual nations; it had triggered World War I. Wilson believed that there had to be a better way, and he believed his League of Nations was the answer. What he didn't know was how other nations would react to his proposal.

So at his direction the executive branch formed a special committee, known only as the Inquiry, to study the matter. Recruiting some of the most knowledgeable and best-connected people from the worlds of American academia and commerce, the Inquiry did more than study. It gathered information from open sources (that is, newspapers and journals) and from informal conversations with well-placed contacts; it probed; it analyzed. And in the end, it helped Wilson to direct the conversation that helped to shape postwar Europe.

The Inquiry was the first real attempt at systematic intelligence gathering and analysis aimed at national policy decisions. Up to this point, intelligence functions operated on a tactical level, dealing with a specific problem or set of conditions, usually military in nature ("How many men are in that trench?"). But the Inquiry's mission was strategic intelligence. It was to determine the attitudes and reactions among nations, through analysis of political, economic, and social conditions. It was a new approach.

Following the Treaty of Versailles, the Inquiry was disbanded. But valuable lessons had been learned. And members of the committee were to play major roles in the shaping of American intelligence and foreign policy through the first half of the twentieth century.

Efforts to obtain tactical intelligence continued between the wars. ONI, MID, and the Department of State pursued independent paths, each focusing on areas of parochial interest, with little sharing of information between the three. Traditional jealousies, rivalries, and one-upmanship plagued the effort. It was only with the gathering of the storm clouds during the 1930s that even a small measure of cooperation would be achieved.

That was to change mightily after the attack on Pearl Harbor in 1941. America was once again in a real shooting war. This time there was no confusion regarding the stakes. As was the case in every armed conflict in which the country found itself, this war did not receive universal support on the home front, but it came as close to unifying the country as any had to that point.

The range and nature of World War II secrets may never be told. Great Britain alone had more than 30,000 people assigned to intelligence operations (communications, counterintelligence, covert operations, analysis, and weapons systems), yet many of their stories are still classified. Government archives in Washington, D.C., still contain massive amounts of documents that remain classified more than 60 years after the fact. Most of the records of the OSS, for example, remain classified. The official histories that have been written are tantalizing more for what has been

left out than for what is revealed. Indeed, much of what is known of OSS activities during the war has come from unofficial sources (memoirs and biographies).

When the leaders and participants wrote their memoirs in the years following the war, references to the secret war were purposely, and perhaps necessarily, heavily edited. It is unfortunate that any insight Winston Churchill might have provided to the use of Ultra (intercepts of German communications provided by Enigma) has been lost; Churchill died two years before the secret of Ultra was made public. When it was made public, in 1967, it was done in violation of Great Britain's Official Secrets Act.

Intelligence operations conducted by the British, indeed by most European nations, were far more established than were those of the United States as the war began. Their tradition of intelligence gathering and "dirty tricks" stretched back several hundred years at that point. The Americans were relative newcomers.

While armies and navies and air forces were slugging it out on islands in the Pacific, jungles in Asia, deserts in Africa, and small towns in Europe, an entirely different war was taking place in the shadows. Totally new technologies were taking the science of SIGINT into totally new areas. The mathematicians hiding in rural estates in the British countryside working on Enigma developed a new science around COMINT. There were engineers spinning dials and watching monitors as they pioneered another new science, that of ELINT. And there were still more engineers and academics intercepting and interpreting foreign instrumentation intelligence (FISINT).

All of this was in addition to assets in place, clandestine submarine landings, and midnight parachute drops into occupied territories providing human intelligence (HUMINT) reports.

DECEPTION AND MISDIRECTION

But at least as important as the gathering of information was the process of spreading disinformation. It was important to know what the other side was thinking; it was at least as important to keep them from knowing what you were thinking. Deception and disinformation were elevated to the level of fine art during World War II.

It was no secret that the Allies intended to invade continental Europe. Personnel and war material were flooding into Great Britain, and Stalin was openly calling for a second front in Europe. What was secret was the timing and location of D-Day.

The idea was to confuse the German High Command. For the invasion to be successful, the Allies knew they would have to quickly establish an area of operations on the continent. The logistics of supplying armies with ammunition, fuel, medicine, food, replacement parts, and reinforcements demanded a secure base. Erwin Rommel, commanding German defenders, knew that any invasion had to be stopped on the beaches. If the Allies were allowed to gain a foothold, Rommel correctly believed, the war would be lost.

The Allies didn't intend to lose, nor did they intend to be stopped on the beaches. To better the chances of a successful invasion, the Germans would be enticed by misdirection to look everywhere other than Normandy for the landings to take place. Operation Fortitude was undertaken.

Fortitude was the name given to the overall deception campaign, and it took a

THE TWENTY COMMITTEE

While the activities of the Twenty Committee of the British intelligence services have passed into history, its legacy survives in the folklore of espionage.

Twenty Committee derived its name from the number of the room in MI6 headquarters that the group originally called home. Even the name was secret. If it was written at all, references were obscured by referring to it in Roman numerals. Thus, *Twenty Committee* became *XX*, and this became *Double Cross*.

CANARIS

German Rear Admiral Wilhelm Canaris. From 1938 until 1944, he headed the bureau for foreign affairs/defense. An active supporter of the resistance movement against Adolf Hitler, he was arrested after his failed assassination attempt on Hitler on July 10, 1944. He was executed on April 9, 1945, in the Nazi concentration camp in Flossenbürg, Germany. (*Corbis*)

Admiral Wilhelm Canaris served as the World War II spymaster for Nazi Germany as head of the vaunted Abwehr (military intelligence), and was a ringleader of the assassination attempt on Adolf Hitler in late July 1944. He was caught by German authorities and tried and executed as a traitor in April 1945, scant weeks before the end of the war in Europe.

But there may be more to the story.

His widow, Erika Canaris, received a pension in her old age. But not from Germany. It had been arranged by Allen Dulles, then head of the CIA. The checks came each month from Uncle Sam.

There's never been a public explanation.

number of different forms. Fortitude-North was aimed at deceiving the Germans into believing the landings would take place in Norway. Fortitude-South pointed to the French port of Calais.

Considerable weight to both programs was provided by the British Twenty Committee. After the war it was revealed that British intelligence had managed to apprehend every Axis agent working out of the British Isles. Not only had they been apprehended, they had been turned into British agents by the Twenty Committee. Throughout the war, these agents continued to report back to Berlin. But the reports they filed were actually authored by British intelligence. The turned agents provided a conduit for misinformation and misdirection to flow to the Abwehr (the German military intelligence service).

No less important than the secrets surrounding D-Day were those surrounding the Manhattan Project. Since the mid-1930s, German physicists had been exploring

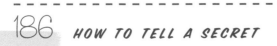

Atomic Bomb Explosion

The Manhattan Project, which led to the development of atomic weapons during World War II, was one of the most closely guarded secrets of the war. The subsequent development of the hydrogen bomb was also shrouded in secrecy. The Soviet Union, through its intelligence network, was aware of breakthroughs almost as soon as they happened. (U.S. Department of Energy)

the possibility of an atomic bomb. It had been deemed theoretically possible, although the problems involved in moving it from theory to a practical working weapon had been monumental. Albert Einstein, the most famous living physicist of the day, wrote a letter to President Roosevelt warning him of the danger and urging him to undertake a program to create the bomb before the Axis did.

In response, the Army Corps of Engineers undertook the development program as a joint effort between the United States and Great Britain. As a cover, it was assigned to the Manhattan Engineering District. In 1942 the Manhattan Project was born.

THE MANHATTAN PROJECT

It was eventually to employ more than 130,000 people and cost nearly $2 billion (in 1942 dollars). Three distinct research and production facilities were built, at Hanford in Washington State, at Oak Ridge in Tennessee, and at Los Alamos in New Mexico. Working together under the direction of army general Leslie Groves (who had just finished building the Pentagon outside Washington, D.C.), the facilities produced three bombs: The Gadget (the first device, set off at Trinity Site in New Mexico, to prove the design worked), Little Boy (dropped on Hiroshima on August 7, 1945) and Fat Man (dropped on Nagasaki on August 9, 1945).

Security surrounding the program was intense. Entire towns were created to house and isolate scientists, technicians, workers, and their families. Everything about the program, including the program's name, was classified. While the existence of the bomb was made public as soon as it was dropped on the Japanese cities, photos were not released until the 1960s. Even today, details of the inner mechanisms remain classified.

Despite the intense security, the project was penetrated by Soviet intelligence. Two of the scientists working on the project, Klaus Fuchs and Theodore Hall, made regular reports on the technological developments to the Soviet Union. A third, Donald Maclean, reported on political developments and plans. Thus, when Truman approached Stalin with the news of the bomb during the Potsdam Conference after Germany's surrender, Stalin already knew. What Truman did not know was the progress the Soviets were making in their own development efforts.

Hiroshima After the Bomb

The Japanese city of Hiroshima had a population of 275,000 in August 1945. Some 240,000 died in the immediate aftermath of the atomic bomb dropped on August 6, 1945. Still, the Japanese High Command refused to surrender until a second bomb was dropped on Nagasaki three days later. The secret was that the Americans had no more bombs to drop after the first two were deployed, and it would take months to produce enough raw material to make more. This Army Signal Corps photograph of Hiroshima's city center was taken two weeks after the attack. (U.S. Department of Energy)

The first Soviet test of an atomic weapon came in August 1949. The weapon detonated was an exact duplicate of Fat Man. The Soviets had reverse-engineered the bomb using information they received from their agents in the United States. Since they had already demonstrated their capabilities for delivering such a weapon

Extra security

The Manhattan Project's S-Site was where the explosives were fabricated and tested; as such, it was the most secret area of the already supersecret Los Alamos compound. A special security badge, such as the one pictured, was required to gain admittance. (Kismet Images)

when they unveiled their long-range bomber, the TU-4, the Western democracies had cause for concern.

A new kind of war was about to be waged. This one wouldn't be a hot, shooting war. It would be a Cold War. Both sides were well aware of the dangers of an all-out conflict. Conventional warfare on a scale to match the mobilization of World War II was now out of the question, as weapons development continued apace and the technology evolved from atomic bombs to nuclear bombs. (It actually takes an atom bomb to set off a hydrogen bomb.) Not only did the number of bombs continue to rise but developments also allowed for their deployment onto the battlefield.

The battlefields of this Cold War were unlike those of previous wars. The superpowers, as they came to be called, carried on their duels through third parties. During the next 35 years, regional conflicts took place in the Middle East (Iran and Afghanistan), in Central America (Guatemala), in Asia (Korea and Vietnam), in Europe (Berlin, Hungary, and Czechoslovakia), and in Africa (the Congo). In each of these conflicts, the United States would (usually covertly) back one side, while the Union of Soviet Socialist Republics would (usually covertly) back the other. It had to be so, if the two superpowers were not to come into direct, open conflict.

Competition, if not conflict, continued through the 1950s. When the Soviet Union continued to test the latest weapons in their nuclear arsenal, the United States needed intelligence as to their capabilities. Lockheed Martin was selected to build a high-altitude aircraft christened the U-2. It was, and is, a spy plane with

TU-4

The Soviet Union's TU-4. A long-range strategic bomber, it was an unauthorized rivet-by-rivet copy of the American B-29 Superfortress. It gave the Soviet Union the capability of reaching the continental United States with nuclear weapons. This declassified image shows that even the Soviet star was positioned exactly where the U.S. Army Air Corps had placed its emblem. (*National Archives and Records Administration*)

The war in the Pacific was nearing the end when the United States first deployed the B-29 Superfortress. It was a propeller-driven long-range bomber with astounding capabilities for payload, speed, and flight duration. The machine employed a number of state-of-the-art, and secret, technologies. And as was the case with many American innovations, the whole thing was classified. Details of the B-29 were not shared with allies from the Soviet Union.

At the time of TU-4's deployment, the Soviet Union was not at war with Japan. Stalin believed, with good reason, that he had his hands full on the battlefields of Europe. He didn't want his forces fighting on two fronts at the same time. So the Soviets were officially neutral for most of the Pacific war.

Under international law, therefore, belligerents from either side who would stray into Soviet territory were to be detained and their equipment impounded.

Soviet territory could not be used as a base of operations for either side to wage war.

On at least four occasions, B-29 crews were forced to ditch in Soviet territory after bombing raids on Japanese targets. The planes had sustained damage and could not return to their home base. The crews were, in fact, detained (although each managed to escape shortly thereafter).

The planes were another matter.

The Soviets had no technology that could match, or even come close to, what was discovered on the B-29s. Stalin personally gave the order to rip the planes apart to learn their secrets. He wanted a Soviet version of the Superfortress.

And he got it. Designated the TU-4, it was a bolt-by-bolt copy of the B-29. One story told of a manufacturing defect in one of the B-29s forced to land in Russia. There was a small hole in the left wing tip, and Soviet engineers couldn't figure out its purpose, since there was no corresponding hole in the right wing tip. It wasn't battle damage, but it had to have been there for a reason. So, orders being orders, each TU-4 had a small hole in the left wing tip.

Rumors of the existence of a Soviet long-range strategic bomber began to leak shortly after the end of the war, but they were discounted. Western intelligence agencies did not believe the Soviets had the scientific know-how to construct such an advanced weapons platform.

The rumors were confirmed, however, in August 1947 when a flight of TU-4s made a public appearance during a patriotic parade in Moscow. With this capability, the Soviet air force could launch strikes, over the North Pole, and reach such American targets as Chicago, New York, or even Los Angeles (on a one-way suicide mission). The situation was made all the more serious in 1949 when the first Soviet atomic bomb was successfully tested.

LEVELS OF INFORMATION CLASSIFICATION

Executive order 12958, issued by President Clinton in April 1995, set the levels of classification used by the various intelligence agencies of the United States:

1. *Top Secret* shall be applied to information, the unauthorized disclosure of which reasonably could be expected to cause exceptionally grave damage to the national security that the original classification authority is able to identify or describe.
2. *Secret* shall be applied to information, the unauthorized disclosure of which reasonably could be expected to cause serious damage to the national security that the original classification authority is able to identify or describe.
3. *Confidential* shall be applied to information, the unauthorized disclosure of which reasonably could be expected to cause damage to the national security that the original classification authority is able to identify or describe.

the ability to fly at an altitude of at least 70,000 feet and over extended distances (many of the capabilities remain classified). The first was delivered in 1955; the most recent (essentially the same design) was placed in service in 1989.

Exactly what this machine can do is a carefully guarded secret. The air force has said that the capabilities have undergone continual upgrades to keep pace with technology. It is known that the aircraft was fitted with state-of-the-art optics and sensing equipment when it was first delivered, and what was then state of the art allowed for the resolution of items the size of a golf ball from that altitude.

The air force needed the machine because it knew it was still years away from the successful launch of a satellite into orbit. They didn't think the Soviets were that far away, and as it turned out, they were right.

The American U-2

These eyes in the skies gave the United States and its allies the ability to spy directly on activities deep within Communist airspace during the Cold War. It flew very high and very fast and was equipped with cameras rather than guns. The pilots who flew the U-2 spy planes were ex-military men who had been "sheep-dipped" and turned into civilian contractors. (National Archives and Records Administration)

Publicly, the space race was about scientific exploration and humankind's need to reach for the stars. And it was, at least in part. But a significant amount of the science to be explored had to do with high-speed communications, communication intercepts, and surveillance. At least half the payloads lifted by the United States during the space race were secret and remain classified; a similar statement about Soviet efforts cannot be made, because even that information is classified.

These high-profile and often public adventures were not the extent of Cold

SHEEP-DIPPED

To give the air forces of the United States and Great Britain a level of deniability, the pilots who flew the U-2 and other spy planes were officially retired from active military service. Legally, they were civilian contractors.

These who have gone through this process of transformation have been "sheep-dipped," a reference to a fox wearing sheep's clothing.

Air America

"First in, last out" was the motto of the CIA's official clandestine airline. From 1946 until 1976, the operation provided logistical and critical mission support to American forces around the world. The organization was so secret that many employees did not know they were on the CIA payroll. A total of 87 people lost their lives in combat while attached to the service. (Courtesy of AirAmerica.org)

War secrets. From its inception by President Truman in 1947, the CIA has conducted covert operations around the world. During the 1960s, for example, the CIA required the services of an independent company to undertake clandestine deliveries of supplies and munitions to various rebel groups around the world. Air America was the result.

Wholly owned and operated by the CIA, Air America flew missions from 1946 until 1976. Its employees were civilian, and in fact, many did not know they

FEDERAL OFFICERS

As you drive past Central Intelligence Agency (CIA) headquarters (the George Bush Center for Intelligence) in Langley, Virginia, just outside Washington, D.C., you will see fences and warnings.

Still, people do tend to pull in. It is usually by mistake, taking a wrong turn or missing an exit. An average weekday may see two or three such guests.

The stays are usually brief. Occupants of the car are stopped at the gates by uniformed security personnel and are asked to identify themselves by producing a driver's license or some other appropriate form of ID. This, along with the car's registration, are run through a database. If all is well, the car is sent along its way with warm wishes for a good day.

What many people do not realize is that those security guards are federal law enforcement officers, with full powers. So if all is not well—say there's an outstanding warrant for arrest—the occupants of the car will be arrested and led away in handcuffs.

It happens several times a month.

---

worked for the government. There had been rumors, of course. But several levels of insulation stood between those on the tarmac and those calling the shots in Langley.

Often undertaking hazardous duties, Air America lost 87 people to combat-related deaths during its history. It was the company's final mission, in 1975, to evacuate the last Americans from South Vietnam.

The battle of disinformation continued, at least through the 1980s. It was no secret that they were spying on us or that we were spying on them. It was in the nature of the information sought that the secrets lie.

The economy of the Soviet Union was in deep trouble. The output of goods and services was falling rapidly; the quality of the goods produced was, by many

The Fall of Saigon

An employee of the Central Intelligence Agency (probably O.B. Harnage) helps Vietnamese evacuees onto an Air America helicopter from the top of 22 Gia Long Street, a half mile from the U.S. embassy, on April 29, 1975. (Corbis/Betteman)

accounts, even worse. And by the middle of the 1980s, Soviet spending on its military was nearly 20% of its gross national product (GNP).

Ronald Reagan, then in the White House, was aware of the situation through information brought to him by the CIA. Analysis showed that the Soviets could not continue on their current path. The decision was reached to bring the Cold War to an end by increasing pressure on the Soviet Union's limited resources. It was much like a game of poker: If the ante was upped, the opponent would be forced to fold and leave the game. It was done largely through a program of disinformation.

First, overtly, the Reagan administration announced plans for a strategic defense initiative. The idea was to build a missile shield, so that incoming warheads would be detected and intercepted while still in space. Critics loudly panned it as a

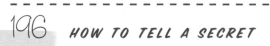

Star Wars approach and claimed it would never work, since available technology wasn't nearly advanced enough to accomplish such a feat.

Whether or not it would work, though, was actually beside the point. The United States was about to significantly increase spending on technologies that could conceivably render Soviet military technologies obsolete. The Soviets couldn't possibly keep up. The United States was spending less than 3% of its GNP on the military; the Soviets were approaching 20%.

The second approach was much more covert. The CIA determined that the Soviets were seeking to acquire infrastructure technology from American companies. Computers were certainly on the list (the Soviets never did develop equivalents of the supercomputers then in use), but so were the technologies involved in robotics and optics and lasers and a host of similar developments.

The decision was made to spread the word through a variety of channels, overt and covert, that the CIA knew all about Soviet efforts to obtain the equipment and underlying technology. The CIA was aware of the dummy companies the Soviets had set up. They knew about purchases through third-party and neutral countries. They knew about clandestine operations to acquire the latest advances.

Rather than thwart these efforts, the CIA encouraged them. Because, the disinformation went, the Soviets weren't getting the whole story. The CIA, you see, had tampered with the equipment. Minor, but significant, flaws had been built into the equipment, so when Soviet engineers would attempt to reproduce the devices they had acquired, they would also reproduce the flaws. Unless, of course, they spent the time to reverse-engineer (rather than just reproduce) everything.

The Soviets hadn't the expertise or the resources to counter what the CIA had reportedly done. And they knew it. The ante had been successfully raised; it was time for the Soviets to fold.

Actually, the CIA hadn't done anything of the kind. It was all disinformation. It was certainly a lot easier, and less expensive, to spread disinformation than it would have been to tamper with the technology.

So it was all a lie. Wasn't it?

CHAPTER 7

SECRETS LOST

September 1862

EVENTS SEEMED TO BE POINTING TO A CONFEDERATE VICTORY in the Civil War. Only four months earlier General Robert E. Lee had assumed command of a force that he dubbed the Army of Northern Virginia. On taking command, he took the army on the offensive, attacking the Federals who were approaching Richmond, the capital of the Confederate States of America, from the South, moving up the peninsula formed by the James and Rappahannock Rivers. In a series of brilliant maneuvers, he brought the Union advance to a standstill and forced the forces under General George McClellan to abandon the campaign and return to Washington, D.C.

The Confederate States of America had adopted essentially a defensive posture up to this point in the war, choosing to be attacked rather than to attack. That was about to change.

Lee proposed to his president, Jefferson Davis, a plan to invade the North. He would move his force to the northwest, swinging around the occupied portion of northern Virginia, and cross the Potomac River and move into Maryland north of the city of Washington, D.C. Several things, he hoped, would be accomplished by such a move. First, it might trigger a revolt in Maryland. The state had decided Southern leanings, and Lee hoped the arrival of Confederate troops would lead to an uprising and the state's secession from the Union. This would effectively cut off Washington, D.C., making it a Federal island in the middle of the Confederacy. A second motive, at least as strong, was a show of force and determination. Not only would an invasion of Northern territory cause serious concern and morale issues in what was left of the Union but it would also demonstrate to England and France that the South was a viable military and, perhaps, political force. The South desperately needed recognition, aid, and, in their wildest dreams, intervention by either or both of the European powers. Both Lee and Davis recognized that the South did not have the resources to sustain a prolonged war.

Robert E. Lee

Perhaps the greatest intelligence blunder of the Civil War was the loss of Robert E. Lee's special order 191, which detailed the disposition of his forces, in plaintext, during the Army of Northern Virginia's first invasion of Union territory. The loss led directly to the Battle of Antietam, the single bloodiest day of the war. (Library of Congress)

George McClellan

George McClellan commanded Union forces during the Battle of Antietam. When presented with a copy of Lee's order, he said, "Here is a paper with which if I cannot whip Bobby Lee I will be willing to go home." He couldn't, and he did. (Library of Congress)

So Lee's command turned north, toward Maryland and, it was hoped, victory. The troops defending Washington, D.C., were aware, at least in a general way, that Lee was on the move, but there was no certainty of where he was headed.

General George McClellan commanded the Army of the Potomac. He knew Lee was marching toward the city of Frederick in Maryland, some 45 miles distant, and gave the command to march. His intention was to intercept Lee as soon as he crossed the Potomac.

Lee had other ideas. He wasn't about to be caught in a trap. So he planned separate advances, two-pronged, that would converge deep within Maryland and be joined there by the forces under Stonewall Jackson.

Detailed instructions, with disposition of troops and proposed routes of advance, were sent via courier to Lee's three corps commanders. These instructions, special order 191, were to be acknowledged and executed without delay.

On the morning of Saturday, September 13, elements of the 27th Indiana

EMANCIPATION PROCLAMATION

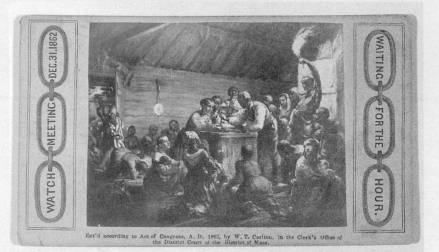

Watch meeting. As the hour of emancipation approached, slaves were expected to gather for celebration. This contemporary image, published in the North at the end of 1862, anticipated one such "watch meeting" taking place in the South. And while Lincoln's Emancipation Proclamation was an important and brilliant document, it actually freed no one when it was issued. *(Library of Congress)*

President Abraham Lincoln is often referred to as "the Great Emancipator," the man who freed the slaves. The Emancipation Proclamation is pointed to as evidence of his actions.

But the Emancipation Proclamation actually freed "all persons

Volunteer Infantry Regiment were making their way north toward Frederick. At about 9:00 AM, they stopped to rest in a field just two miles south of the city. The trampled ground and campfire rings were ample evidence that a large body of men had camped in this field the previous night. Those men must have been Confederates, since the 27th Indiana was in the vanguard of Union troops.

held as slaves within any State or designated part of a State, the people whereof shall then be in rebellion against the United States."

Slavery was legal in a number of states that remained loyal to the Union during the Civil War (Kentucky, Tennessee, Delaware, and Maryland). Since those states were not in rebellion, those slaves were not freed. Technically, it freed the slaves of the South, but practically, Lincoln's edicts had no legal standing there, since those states did not recognize the authority of Washington, D.C. Since the proclamation did not originate in Richmond, the states of the Confederacy chose to ignore it.

What the proclamation did do, however, was prevent either England or France from recognizing the Confederate States of America as an independent country.

Neither country could do so without appearing to support the institution of slavery.

Lincoln's second accomplishment with the Emancipation Proclamation was a shift in the emphasis of the rationale for the war. Before it was issued, the war had been a struggle to preserve the Union. Once it had been issued, however, the war became a moral crusade to free human beings from bondage.

As Federal armies advanced through the Confederate States of America, slaves were freed using the Emancipation Proclamation as the legal basis. And one by one, the loyal Northern states where slavery was still legal (except Kentucky) outlawed the practice. It wasn't until the passage of the 13th Amendment to the Constitution in 1865 that slavery was permanently abolished from the United States.

As the men were relaxing, one noticed a piece of paper lying on the ground. He had just discovered the biggest security blunder of the war. Picking up the paper, he was very pleased to discover that it was wrapped around three fresh cigars. He was much more interested in the cigars than in the paper. His sergeant, however, was interested in the paper. It was a copy of special order 191. Written in plaintext, it laid bare Lee's entire plan. The orders had been left behind when the Confederates went on the march. Quickly it made its way up the chain of command, and by noon it was in the hands of General McClellan and his staff. It was like a gift: the marching orders for the Army of Northern Virginia for the next four days.

So now McClellan knew that Lee had split his forces into three columns, and that these were now spread out, now more than 20 miles apart and moving away from one another. He knew where each was headed. He knew that if he moved rapidly, he could engage and overcome each force independently. He knew where and when they were going to converge.

"Here is a paper with which if I cannot whip Bobby Lee I will be willing to go home," McClellan reportedly told his staff. Never before had a Union commander enjoyed such an intelligence coup.

Unfortunately, it took McClellan four days to get the Army of the Potomac moving. By that time, Lee had managed to bring most of his command together. The two armies did meet, but instead of engaging them piecemeal, McClellan was forced to take them all at once at a little creek called the Antietam, just outside the town of Sharpsburg in Maryland. It was the single bloodiest day of the Civil War, with more than 23,000 men killed, wounded, or missing. Technically, the battle was a draw; strategically, it was a Union victory, since it forced Lee to retreat back to Virginia, and it gave Lincoln an excuse to issue his Emancipation Proclamation.

SECRETS REVEALED

Herbert O. Yardley, a noted American cryptologist, started his career as a telegraph operator for the railroads before joining the State Department prior to the outbreak of World War I. Working the night shift, and stationed in the basement with the machines receiving incoming cables from embassies around the world, Yardley would amuse himself by breaking the diplomatic codes then in place. So successful was he at it that he was reprimanded for unauthorized access to the information flowing across his desk. It was far above his pay scale to decipher the messages and learn their contents. Nevertheless, he came to be viewed as a bit of a wizard when it came to matters of cryptology.

Censor's Office

The U. S. Army's censor's office in World War I France tested suspicious materials for secret writing before releasing letters to the mail. (Library of Congress)

With the outbreak of the war, Yardley talked his way into a lieutenant's commission and a posting with the American Expeditionary Force as head of the new cryptology section. While in France, his group built on his reputation by developing new codes for the army and by breaking a number of enemy ciphers. He also headed the group that developed new invisible inks along with detection methods for uncovering the enemy's invisible inks. After the armistice, Yardley and his group remained in France, performing duties on behalf of the American delegation to the peace conference.

After the war, and the usual rush to reduce military spending, Yardley's position as cryptologist extraordinaire for the U.S. government was in real jeopardy. But the product his group produced was considered so valuable that he succeeded in his efforts to form a new agency jointly funded by the state department and the war department. Officially dubbed the Cipher Bureau, it was to be a secret organization. The American Black Chamber was born.

Beginning in late 1919 and working from offices in New York City, Yardley's group had a string of successes. Yardley himself focused on the codes employed by Japanese commercial and diplomatic agencies. It was widely believed in the two departments serviced by the Cipher Bureau that Japan would emerge as America's new threat. The worth of the new group was proven during negotiations over a new naval treaty in 1921.

The United States and Great Britain wanted to limit the size of the growing

Herbert O. Yardley

Commissioned a lieutenant in the U.S. Army during World War I, Yardley led American efforts at cryptanalysis during the war. He later led the joint State Department-War Department cryptanalysis program, and he told all the secrets when he wrote a best-selling book, The American Black Chamber. The debate as to whether he was hero or villain continues. (National Archives and Records Administration)

Japanese Navy and were pushing for a ratio of capital ships (battlewagons and heavy cruisers). Japan wanted the ratio to be 10:10:7. And while the United States and Great Britain had no problem with parity, neither was willing to accept such a high figure from Japan. Having broken the Japanese system, Yardley was able to supply American representatives with Japan's complete strategy, including their minimum acceptable terms. The negotiations proved arduous, and Japan was surprised by the determination shown by the American team. With their foreknowledge and through tough negotiating stands, the United States was able to push Japan to the very lower limit of what it was willing to accept. A final ratio of 5:5:3 was agreed on. Japan was less than happy but believed that the ratio was the best it could get.

Within the somewhat limited circles of the American intelligence community at the time, Yardley was a hero. He himself was the star performer; his group was America's secret weapon.

That was to have been the Cipher Bureau's high-water mark, however. The war department already had two functioning agencies (the Army Signal Corps' MID and the Navy's ONI) performing SIGINT activities, and it chose to ignore the Cipher Bureau. The State Department still had no coordinated effort to collect and analyze intelligence. At the same time, the volume of intercepted diplomatic traffic that the bureau was receiving was falling rapidly. The cable companies that handled overseas traffic showed growing reluctance to cooperate with the government by delivering copies of the traffic, for fear of jeopardizing their business relationships with foreign governments. This growing reluctance was underscored by a 1927 act of Congress that made it a federal crime to intercept or disclose the contents of electronic communications. As the volume of work decreased, so did the staff of the Cipher Bureau; by 1929 only five people remained on the payroll.

Henry L. Stimson was the new secretary of state under President Herbert Hoover, and when he was briefed on the existence and function of the Cipher Bureau in May 1929, he reportedly reacted with unqualified condemnation. He thought it was both illegal and improper, and he ordered an immediate termination of the State Department's share of the funding, and the Cipher Bureau was forced to cease operations.

Yardley took home two boxes bulging with classified documents, including the

THE MOST SECRET MUSEUM

The world of secrets is actually fairly well documented and on display.

The National Security Agency (NSA) runs the National Cryptologic Museum just outside the gates of its headquarters in Fort Meade, Maryland, about a half hour's drive north of Washington, D.C. Admission is free and open to the public.

The Central Intelligence Agency (CIA) also boasts an impressive collection of memorabilia and spy gadgets. Admittance to the museum, while free, is limited to current and past employees, however. But online tours are available by visiting the official CIA Web site and following the links there.

While the Federal Bureau of Investigation (FBI) never had a museum per se, tours of the headquarters (with views of displayed items of historical interest) had been a popular activity for people visiting Washington, D.C. since the building opened in 1977. A general tour was open to the public; a special tour could be arranged by a call to a member of the House of Representatives or the Senate. The building was closed to public tours after the terrorist attacks of September 11, 2001, but the official Web site contains information on the agency's history.

Perhaps the most secret museum may be found in a far back corner of the headquarters of the U.S. Secret Service in Washington, D.C., just a few short blocks from the White House. It is not open to the public. The museum's artifacts are not displayed online. The room is locked even to employees.

Included in that collection are samples of counterfeit currency and items related to presidential assassinations (the pistol that killed William McKinley) and assassination attempts (the back door of the limousine, complete with bullet holes, that carried Ronald Reagan to the hospital after he was shot).

details of behind-the-scenes activities during the Washington Naval Conference. He later wrote *The American Black Chamber*, an account of the history and successes of the Cipher Bureau, with specifics regarding the bureau's mission and techniques. And it told the story of the negotiations of the naval treaty in minute detail, quoting encrypted cables and outlining strategies. Officially and publicly, the U.S. government denied that such a thing as a Cipher Bureau ever existed and said the entire story was a fabrication.

Yardley continued his writing career, producing three spy novels during the 1930s (one of which became the movie *Rendezvous* in 1935). As a follow-up to this first book, he wrote *Japanese Diplomatic Codes: 1921–1922* in 1933, but it was immediately seized by the government and was not declassified until 1979. During World War II, he worked briefly for Canada and later for the Nationalist Chinese as a cryptanalyst for Chiang Kai-shek. His last literary foray, which met with modest success, came with the publication of *The Education of a Poker Player* in 1958. Yardley died the following year and is buried in Arlington National Cemetery. He has since received a place in the Hall of Honor at the NSA headquarters at Fort Meade in Maryland and has been inducted into the Military Intelligence Hall of Fame.

Such honors do not come to every teller of secrets, particularly when those tellers were once charged with keeping the secrets. For some very good and obvious reasons, many choose to remain anonymous.

Yardley, keeper of secrets, gained fame as a teller of secrets.

SECRETS DISCERNED: MAGIC OPERATIONS

The opening months of 1942 saw some of the darkest days for Allied forces in the Pacific. The Imperial Japanese government, led by upper-echelon members of the military, had developed a vision in the 1930s of a network of interdependent Asian countries free of Western influences and colonial governments. This vision was called the Greater East Asia Co-Prosperity Sphere, and it was to include the countries of east Asia and Southeast Asia. The immediate goal was to remove the French, British, Dutch, and American colonial regimes. The long-range goal was to

Pearl Harbor

December 7, 1941, the "day that will live in infamy," saw the Japanese attack on the American naval base at Pearl Harbor, Hawaii, and the Army Air Corps' installation at Hickam Field, Hawaii. Magic told the diplomats, politicians, and military commanders in Washington, D.C., that something was coming, but the warning was sent via commercial telegraph and arrived too late to be effective. (National Archives and Records Administration)

replace those regimes with Japanese puppet governments. The attack on Pearl Harbor was merely the opening salvo of making that vision a reality. It was followed immediately with a series of lightning attacks, all designed to establish and expand the sphere.

Guam fell on December 10; Wake Island, on December 23. The French possessions in Southeast Asia were attacked on December 8; it took less than a week for the Japanese Army to take control. Malaysia also came under attack on December 8,

World War II Occupation Currency

After the rapid expansion of the Greater East Asia Co-prosperity Sphere in 1941-1942, the Japanese government issued occupation currency in the conquered territories. These notes were issued in the Philippines. (Kismet Images)

and after the sinking of two of Britain's capital ships, HMS *Prince of Wales* and HMS *Repulse*, it, too, fell. The surviving defenders of Malaysia fell back on Singapore, considered to be impenetrable; it wasn't. It held for two months, but it fell in February. Christmas Day saw the surrender of Hong Kong. The Dutch East Indies came under attack at the start of the New Year, and by March, its rich oil fields were in Japanese hands. Combined American and Filipino forces on Corregidor Island in Manila Bay surrendered on April 9, signaling the fall of the Philippines. And Siam, gateway to both India and China, was attacked in January and in Japanese hands by May. All the while, the Japanese Army was in control of Korea and had made significant inroads into China.

In less than 6 months, the Greater East Asia Co-Prosperity Sphere encompassed nearly 10% of the globe. Worse, from the Allies' perspective, it didn't look like there was any way to stop it from growing further. Japan had crushed every force it had encountered on land and sea, and the Allies had little left to throw against it.

The Greater East Asia Co-Prosperity Sphere

Within six months of the December 1941 attack on American forces based in Hawaii, the "Greater East Asia Co-Prosperity Sphere" (the name given the territory conquered by Japan) included nearly 10% of the globe. It encompassed the Korean Peninsula, Manchuria, parts of China, the countries of Southeast Asia, the Philippines, Indonesia, much of Oceania, and even the southernmost of the Aleutian Islands of Alaska. (Kismet Images)

AN UNFORTUNATE TITLE

Ernest J. King was named chief of naval operations for the U.S. Navy shortly after the attack on Pearl Harbor. A graduate of the United States Naval Academy at Annapolis and a veteran of the Spanish-American War, he was an experienced and well-respected officer. His offices were in Washington, D.C. and later in the newly completed Pentagon. As ranking officer he was a member of the Joint Chiefs of staff, and he was responsible for directing naval operations world-wide throughout the war.

One of his first acts on assuming command was to change his acronym. Up to that point, the official title of his position, commander-in-chief of the U.S. fleet, had been abbreviated to CINCUS (pronounced "sink us"). He changed it to COMINCH.

The horrible realization dawned that there was almost nothing standing between Tokyo and San Francisco other than open and largely uncontested ocean. The United States could muster a few aircraft carriers, a handful of combat-ready ships, and a few scattered outposts on isolated Pacific Islands. The entire West Coast of the United States was vulnerable to attack and invasion.

The Japanese never intended to invade the continental United States. The overall Japanese strategic plan had been to expand the Greater East Asia Co-Prosperity Sphere to the point where they knew that their home islands would be safe from attack, to consolidate their new territories, and then sue for peace on terms they would dictate.

But the Japanese high command never anticipated that it would go so well, that their plans would be carried out so quickly and at so little cost. Casualty rates of men and equipment were forecast at 25%, but the actual numbers were a fraction of that figure. In six months Japan had accomplished what it had set out to do, and it still retained the bulk of its military might.

A new, and somewhat improvised, strategy was adopted. On the southern flank, Japan would attack Port Moresby in Papua, New Guinea. A foothold there, only 400 miles from Australia, would give Japan access to additional resources, provide a base from which to attack either Australia or India, and concentrate on what was left of British and Commonwealth land forces, with the potential for their annihilation.

To the north, another plan was put in place. First, the Japanese Army would invade the Aleutian Islands. The islands were American territory, a chain extending from Alaska some 1,200 miles into the Pacific. They held little strategic value, but since they were American territory, it was believed that an invasion would draw forces for their defense. And that was the idea. Japan didn't particularly want the islands; they wanted a diversion.

The real prize was Midway Island. Midway, actually an atoll, lies near the geographic center of the North Pacific, roughly 1,100 miles north of Hawaii. Japan hoped that an attack would draw what was left of the American navy into a pitched battle where it would be seriously outgunned. Thus, with both Midway and part of the Aleutians in Japanese hands, and with its navy in shambles, the United States would be forced to accept Japan's peace terms.

Japan got its battle, but it didn't turn out quite as the high command had planned it. What Japan did not know was that the Americans had some "magic" on their side.

The United States had been reading Japanese military, commercial, and diplomatic communications for nearly 20 years (a practice known as "Magic"). Penetration of the system wasn't complete, but somewhere between 85% and 90% of any given message could be translated to English plaintext in a matter of hours.

Station Hypo was the code name of magic operations in Hawaii. It was housed in the basement of an administration building in the navy yard at Pearl Harbor. A long, windowless room was home to the men of the Combat Intelligence Unit. Casual visitors were not welcome and were so informed by the 24-hour armed guard. If visitors managed to get past the guard, they would still have to deal with a set of locked and barred gates at the top of the stairs and yet another at the bottom.

Lieutenant Commander Joseph Rochefort was in command of Station Hypo at the time. Rochefort had assumed command in May 1941, and together with two other cryptanalysts and a crew of technicians, clerks, and Japanese language experts, he was responsible for COMINT in the Pacific theater.

The sheer volume of intercepted traffic that came to this room was overwhelming. The complement assigned, roughly 30 officers and enlisted men, could not possibly decode all the messages into English plaintext. Even the International Business Machine (IBM) tabulators with their stacks of punch cards couldn't do it all. The focus before the war was on the messages transmitted in the Japanese Flag Officer's code.

Everything changed with the attack. Priority was given to Rochefort's command: space, equipment, and personnel. With the shortages of all three in the days and weeks following the attack, that was the true indication of the importance placed on the operation by the top brass.

Rochefort needed people for administrative duties and as punch-card operators to keep the raw data flowing into his IBM machines. So they gave him a brass band. It had been the band stationed on the USS *California*, which was now sitting on the bottom of the harbor. The musicians from the *California* were up to their new task, and several became more than competent cryptanalysts.

The operation had expanded rapidly, but so had the pressure to produce. Magic

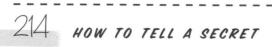

had empowered the Americans to translate intercepted communications, but the Japanese were using an elaborate code word system in addition to encryption. Rochefort's code breakers were able to translate the intercepts into plaintext, but without a dictionary of the code words being used, the full meaning could not be stated with certainty.

When operational orders for the invasion of the Aleutian Islands and the attack on Midway were transmitted from Tokyo, the Japanese had no reason to suspect that the Americans were reading their radio traffic. Indeed, their rapid progress across the Pacific would lead them to believe that their codes had *not* been broken.

It was late May when the orders went out. The transmission detailed the plans, including dates, times, and coordinates, for an attack on Midway Island.

Rochefort's crew labored mightily with the intercept. The IBM tabulators were crunching through the code groups, looking for matches with known code words. The work was slow, and while Station Hypo was able to decipher the majority of the

MIDWAY

The Battle of Midway. The Battle of Midway marked the turning point for the Pacific theater during World War II. An inspired piece of deception by Station Hypo in Honolulu provided the missing piece of the puzzle that allowed the Allies to surprise and overwhelm the Japanese fleet. The USS *Yorktown* is shown under heavy fire during the battle. (*National Archives and Records Administration*)

The true impact of the Battle of Midway was not that the Pacific atoll had been denied to the enemy. In fact, it wouldn't have made much difference to the Allied cause or the outcome

text, there were gaps in the translation, the most significant of which was the actual target. The orders referred to the target as *FS*, a code word that hadn't yet been encountered.

A captured Imperial Japanese Navy map seemed to indicate that *FS* was the grid where Midway was located, but this was more supposition than anything else. Admiral Chester Nimitz, commander in chief in the Pacific, needed more than supposition before he would commit the few remaining forces protecting the West Coast.

There was simply too much at stake. He demanded confirmation of the code word.

of the war if the Japanese had taken it.

Once taken, the island would have been a logistical nightmare. It is totally isolated in its mid-ocean position, well over 2,000 miles from the islands of Japan—or any base of reinforcements or supplies, for that matter. And while the surface navy of the United States had been seriously damaged by the Pearl Harbor attack, the submarine navy was untouched. One or two submarines operating in tandem would have imposed a naval blockade, sinking any ships that dared to approach. Resupply by air would have tasked the Japanese Navy even further.

The strategic importance of the Battle of Midway was that it leveled the playing field. Japan had sent a sizable portion of its available fleet on the mission in an attempt to overwhelm American naval forces. The losses it sustained to its combat effectiveness could not be replaced, whereas the United States was just gearing up.

The battle marked the turning point of the war in the Pacific. From that point onward Allied forces went on the offensive; Japanese forces were forced into a defensive posture. It was now only a matter of time until the Japanese were defeated.

What Rochefort did next was a bit of world-class subterfuge. By secure cable, the garrison at Midway was instructed to transmit a bogus message. They were to report, in plaintext via radio, that their freshwater distillation plant had broken down. He expected the Japanese, monitoring the traffic, would pick up the report and pass it along.

It worked.

On May 25, two days after Midway sent its false report, Magic intercepted and decoded a Japanese report stating that FS was running short of freshwater. The admiral had his confirmation. In fact, because of the efforts of Rochefort's organization

BIGOT

BIGOT-in-Chief. President Franklin Roosevelt knew all the secrets. (*U.S. Department of Transportation*)

If you were a BIGOT in 1944, that was about as high as you could go in terms of security clearances.

Only those who were in the know regarding one of the Allies' most closely guarded secrets of the war were given BIGOT clearances. They would be privy to the date, time, and location of the invasion of Normandy (D-Day, called "Operation Overlord").

Even the term was classified. It originated from the stamp placed on orders to proceed to Gibraltar in anticipation of the invasion of North Africa in November 1942. Those orders were stamped "To Gib." Reverse the flow from North Africa to Europe, and you've got BIGOT.

in translating multiple transmissions, Nimitz probably had a better idea of the overall Japanese plan than did many Japanese ship captains.

Knowing it was a diversionary tactic, Nimitz chose to ignore the invasion of the Aleutian Islands. Instead he focused his forces on Midway. He sent his three remaining heavy aircraft carriers to a point where they could ambush the approaching, and unsuspecting, Japanese fleet.

The Japanese had been correct in their estimation of the strength of the remaining American forces: They were heavily outnumbered. But the combination of

Magic intelligence and Nimitz's strategy allowed those forces to impose maximum punishment on the enemy. Magic intercepts provided the intelligence and firm grounding that allowed Nimitz to exercise his skills to turn back the Japanese onslaught.

What Rochefort and Station Hypo had been able to accomplish was a subtle but significant shift in emphasis: Rather than working to discover the enemy's secrets, they enticed the enemy into just telling them. It turns out that many, if not most, secrets that come to light have done so in this way.

SECRETS LEAKED: WATERGATE

The publication of *All the President's Men* by Carl Bernstein and Bob Woodward in 1974 sparked a quest to discover the identity of a primary source of information for the reporters.

The book detailed the story of the two investigative reporters, then working for the *Washington Post*, as they followed clues and uncovered the activities surrounding the break-in at the Democratic National Committee headquarters in the Watergate complex in Washington, D.C., prior to the 1972 presidential election. One of the reporters (Woodward) claimed he had an anonymous source, highly placed within the executive department. Whenever the reporters came to a dead end in their investigations, they would turn to this source for information and clues that would put them back on the right course. In the book they referred to this source as Deep Throat.

Deep Throat's identity was a carefully guarded secret. Reportedly, only Woodward and Bernstein and the *Post*'s managing editor, Ben Bradlee, knew who Deep Throat was, and they were bound to secrecy by a journalistic code to protect sources' identities.

Speculation was rampant. Graduate courses at respectable universities were built around the mystery. There was speculation in the media and speculation by some of the participants in the Watergate scandal. There was even speculation that Deep Throat was not a single source but a composite—a literary construct to hide the identities of multiple sources.

Deep Throat himself came forward in 2005. He was retired, ailing, and living in northern California. Mark Felt had been a career FBI officer who rose to the highest levels of the agency. In the early 1970s he joined J. Edgar Hoover's inner circle of assistants and was effectively the number-two man in the agency at the time of Hoover's death in 1972. He had anticipated that he would be named the new director after Hoover's death, but he was passed over by the Nixon White House in favor of L. Patrick Gray.

It might have been bitterness over the loss of the position, it might have been patriotism, or it might have been a combination of the two that led Felt to leak information on the ongoing Watergate investigation to Woodward. Whatever the case, Felt was in a position to know where the FBI investigation stood and what was being revealed. His desk was the control point for all matters relating to Watergate. All reports and every scrap of information came to him.

Woodward and Bernstein maintained that Deep Throat was not a primary source of information but a confirming source. In other words, if the reporters had

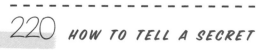

a piece of the puzzle from one source, they could turn to Deep Throat for confirmation, but Deep Throat would not provide any fresh information. This might have been a bit of misdirection. The reporters were well aware that on June 19, 1972 (two days after the break-in), Felt told Woodward that one of the burglars was arrested with an address book containing the White House phone number of E. Howard Hunt. The first published connection between the break-in and the White House can be traced directly to Felt.

Following his revelation, Felt received both praise and criticism. The praise came from those who believed Felt acted out of patriotism and respect for the rule of law. Criticism came from those who pointed out that Felt, charged with keeping secrets, had betrayed the trust placed in him, and the oath he took, on receiving his security clearances.

Alexander P. Butterfield was another figure in the Watergate story with a good secret. On July 16, 1973, he told the Senate committee investigating the Watergate affair that the White House had a secret taping system. The Oval Office was bugged. The Cabinet Room was bugged. So was the president's hideaway office in the Old Executive Office Building. And several cabins at Camp David. And the White House telephone system. Very few people knew about the system, fewer than 10; Butterfield was one of them because he had the system installed and maintained.

It was installed in 1970, at about the midpoint of President Nixon's first term, and there was nothing nefarious about it. The president simply wanted an accurate record made of his tenure in the White House. According to Butterfield, Nixon was thinking of history. He wanted to be sure that historians and scholars would have an accurate picture of his presidency. He wanted the record to include not just the dry facts but also the color and tone of the times. He felt this could best be done with a taping system, so that speech patterns and even inflections would be available. Nixon also believed, perhaps correctly, that a person sitting in the corner taking notes on everything that was said would stifle conversations and creativity. Surreptitious taping, on the other hand, would capture every word without making anyone uncomfortable.

Butterfield believed the system needed to be simple because, in his words, the president was "technologically inept and couldn't be trusted to work a toggle

Nixon and Staff

Richard M. Nixon, thirty-seventh president of the United States, at his desk in the Oval Office, confers with members of his staff (from left: H. R. Haldeman, Dwight Chapin, and John Ehrlichman. (National Archives and Records Administration)

switch." If the president had to remember to punch buttons to turn the system on and off, it just wasn't going to work. So it was automated and would start to record whenever the president was in earshot. To ensure that the sound was being captured, six microphones were hidden on or in the president's desk. Others were placed in lamps in the Oval Office. Similar arrangements were made in his other offices and in the Cabinet Room.

Nearly 3,700 hours of conversations were recorded while the system was in place. And while the committee was certainly interested in learning about all this, what it really wanted to know was whether the president had incriminated himself in a crime. It turned out that he had.

During a meeting with his chief of staff, H. R. Haldeman, on June 23, 1972, less than a week after the break-in, President Nixon discussed ways of getting the FBI to tone down its investigation. That is called obstruction of justice, and that is a federal crime. As far as the Congress was concerned, it was a "high crime" and was cause for impeachment.

The meeting was on tape. At least one of the six microphones hidden in the president's desk had recorded the entire conversation. A battle over releasing the tapes, particularly the tape of that meeting, raged in the courts. The White House claimed executive privilege, which would allow the tapes to remain the personal property of the president. Congress begged to disagree. By this time a special prosecutor was filing briefs and demanding access to the evidence, too.

FELT AGAIN

During their meeting in the Oval Office on June 23, 1972, President Nixon and his chief of staff, H. R. Haldeman, discussed various strategies that could be employed to divert the team of investigators from the Federal Bureau of Investigation probing the Watergate fiasco. One of the ideas proposed was to suggest that a Central Intelligence Agency (CIA) connection existed and to hint that matters of national security were involved. The rationale was to be that the burglars were Cuban and that they had been on the CIA payroll at one point in connection with the failed Bay of Pigs invasion some years earlier.

Nixon and Haldeman believed this was possible because they had a high-level ally at the FBI. Haldeman made a note to call their ally, a man by the name of Mark Felt.

The Supreme Court issued its decision: The White House was to release the tapes. The president had no choice. But he knew that as soon as the transcript of the meeting was made public, clear evidence of his guilt would be in every newspaper around the world. The press labeled it "the Smoking Gun Tape." The day it was released, the president signed his letter of resignation.

Richard Nixon, secret-keeper-in-chief, became the secret-teller-in-chief when the "Smoking Gun" tape was made public.

SECRETS RECORDED: MONICAGATE

Amid the general hue and cry that accompanied daily coverage and analysis of the developing Watergate scandal were commentaries bemoaning the fact that the president's paranoia had permeated the White House, and it led him to go so far as to secretly tape those who would meet with him in the Oval Office or speak with him on the phone.

The practice of covert recording of conversations and telephone calls in the White House actually started with President Roosevelt in 1940. Every president, from Roosevelt to Nixon, had recording systems in place. In most cases the goal appears to have been historical accuracy. Roosevelt in particular was disturbed about being misquoted and having his off-the-cuff comments taken and repeated out of context. But with the cumbersome equipment available at the time, he seems not to have employed his system to a great extent.

Not all clandestine taping schemes have sprung from such high-minded ideals, of course. In 1996, Linda Tripp started down a path that would lead through the White House to an independent council's office and eventually meander through the halls of Congress.

Tripp first came to the White House in an administrative staff position during the administration of George H. W. Bush in 1989. With the coming of the new Clinton administration in 1993, Tripp was reassigned from the White House to the public affairs office of the Pentagon. It was while working in this office that she developed a friendship with another staff member who had just come over from the White House, a young woman named Monica Lewinsky.

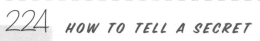

PRESIDENTIAL RECORDINGS

The first covert recording system in the White House was installed during the administration of President Franklin Roosevelt in 1940. The practice continued through subsequent administrations until President Gerald Ford ordered the system removed when he took the oath of office in 1974.

The tapes are legally the property of the U.S. government and are in the care of the National Archives and Records Administration. Since many of these recordings contain conversations dealing with material that may still be classified, care is being taken with their release. And as a practical matter, there is so much material there that it may be many years before all of it has been made public.

A quick overview:

PRESIDENT	HOURS OF RECORDINGS
Franklin Roosevelt	8 hours (all released)
Harry Truman	10 hours (all released)
Dwight Eisenhower	
As president	4.5 hours (all released)
Prepresidential	10 hours (all released)
John F. Kennedy	260 hours (total)
	195 hours (released)
Lyndon Johnson	800 hours (total)
	550 hours (released)
Richard Nixon	3,700 hours (total)
	2,019 hours (released)

Despite a 24-year age difference, the two women bonded and began to socialize outside the office. As they came to know each other, they exchanged confidences. One of these confidences from Lewinsky was astonishing. She told Tripp that while working as an intern at the White House, she had conducted an illicit affair with the president. The affair had not been physically consummated, according to Lewinsky, but it had come pretty close.

Tripp had a friend who was a literary agent in New York City. She thought that there might be a book in all of this, and she started to take notes. For the sake of accuracy, she decided to tape some of the telephone conversations she had with Lewinsky. Since she, like Nixon before her, didn't wish to stifle the conversations, she decided that keeping the tapes secret would be a good idea.

President Clinton at the time was embroiled in a civil suit filed by a former employee of the state of Arkansas, alleging sexual harassment while he was still governor of Arkansas. As part of that suit, depositions and affidavits were being taken and filed from a number of people who might have even tangential knowledge of the circumstances or who were material witnesses to the president's conduct. Both Linda Tripp and Monica Lewinsky received subpoenas to provide testimony.

Lewinsky was concerned that her relationship with the president would become a matter of public record. On a number of occasions she spoke with Tripp to ensure that their testimony matched and to urge Tripp not to reveal her secret tryst. Lewinsky also told Tripp that her affidavit would deny any romantic or physical relationship with the President.

Tripp had it all on tape.

While all this was going on, the president was also under investigation by an independent council, Kenneth Starr, who was probing a failed real estate deal in Arkansas. Tripp went to Starr and, after receiving a promise of immunity from prosecution, revealed all and turned the tapes over to Starr's office. It was almost enough, but not quite.

Starr instructed Tripp to have yet another meeting with Lewinsky. This time, however, Tripp was to wear a concealed microphone that would transmit the conversation to FBI officers who would be nearby and listening. Tripp called Lewinsky and arranged to meet for lunch at a Washington-area shopping mall. For three hours Tripp guided the conversation through the entire episode, enticing Lewinsky to review all the details of the entire affair and her subsequent attempts to keep it quiet.

Days later Lewinsky was visited by FBI agents and members of Starr's staff. She was taken to a hotel room and confronted with the evidence. Filing a sworn affidavit that contains false information (as she had done with regard to the civil suit) was perjury. Enlisting the aid of Tripp to hide the fact of her false affidavit was conspiracy. Attempting to convince Tripp to change her testimony to confirm Lewinsky's was suborning perjury in a witness. Lewinsky was in deep trouble with the feds.

Lewinsky had no choice other than to confirm what was already on the tapes and to provide additional detail and physical evidence. By doing so, she provided proof to Starr that the president had committed perjury in his testimony in the civil suit.

Starr compiled all this evidence and presented it to the House of Representatives. In his official capacity as independent prosecutor, he believed the president had committed perjury. He left it to members of the House to decide whether this fit the requirements for "high crimes and misdemeanors" that the Constitution dictated as grounds for impeachment. The House thought it did and passed articles of impeachment against William Jefferson Clinton, forty-second president of the United States. The State of Arkansas, meanwhile, found Clinton in contempt of civil court for supplying misleading answers in the civil suit, and he was fined $91,000. The court referred the matter to the Arkansas Supreme Court. Rather than contest the matter, Clinton voluntarily surrendered his license to practice law. He then made an out-of-court payment of $850,000 in settlement of the civil suit.

The danger came from secret-keepers who couldn't keep a secret. Lewinsky, primary holder of the secret, had to share it with someone. The someone she chose just happened to be taping the whole thing.

SECRETS PUBLISHED: THE PENTAGON PAPERS

Entire careers have been built around secret-keepers who can't keep a secret. The "highly placed and reliable" sources often quoted in newspaper exposés often fall into this category. While the investigative reporters who write and publish the stories do tend to probe and dig and verify details, most of their time is spent simply making themselves available to the secret-keepers. The theory is that someone somewhere has something they want to get off their chest.

Sometimes the motivation for telling is truly altruistic. Sometimes the telling will further the ambitions of the keeper. Sometimes the motivations are a complex combination of many motivations. From the investigative journalists' point of view, however, the motivation is secondary; what's important is the secret.

The First Amendment to the Constitution of the United States guarantees freedom of the press. It states that the government may not interfere with a news entity's right to publish any news or information that it deems to be in the public interest. Subsequent decisions by the Supreme Court have extended these protections to reporters. By tradition, then, neither the reporters nor their employers are legally taken to task when classified information is published. These First Amendment protections, however, do not extend to the sources of the information. Disclosing classified information to outside sources is a serious offense.

In 1971 the *New York Times* acquired documents relating to the conduct of the war in Vietnam from an employee of the U.S. Department of Defense. Formally entitled *United States–Vietnam Relations, 1945–1967: A Study Prepared by the Department of Defense*, it was 47 volumes and 7,000 pages of top-secret information that had been prepared for study within the Pentagon. This report, which came to be known as the Pentagon Papers, detailed decades of secret, and potentially illegal, operations and activities of various departments within the U. S. government. Since it also showed how the United States had expanded the conflict from Vietnam into the neighboring country of Laos at a time when the Johnson administration was making very public noises about scaling back the war, it cast direct doubt on the credibility of government pronouncements.

Shortly after the *New York Times* started publishing extracts of the documents, the *Washington Post* (which had acquired its own copy of the report from the same source) started its series. Lawyers from the Department of Justice moved swiftly, through court orders, to have publication cease. The case went to the U.S. Supreme Court.

In a 6–3 decision issued on June 26, 1971, the Supreme Court lifted the publication ban and upheld the right of the newspapers to continue publication. It was hailed as a victory for First Amendment rights, since it cleared the way for newspapers to publish information that, in their opinion, was deemed in the public interest.

But the decision did nothing to protect the tellers of the secrets. They were still bound by oath to protect their secrets. And their telling of the secrets, "leaks," could have profound effects on national security.

It was in direct response to the publication of the Pentagon Papers that a new office was established within the executive branch. Headquartered in a basement room of the Old Executive Office Building next to the White House, a small group was tasked with tracking down and stopping the leaks. Some say it was an inside joke, while others maintained it was part of the overall security of the group; whatever the case, a hand-written sign appeared on the office door one morning announcing that this was the Plumbers' office.

These were very serious men and they were performing what they believed to be a vital government service. The group consisted of current and former CIA officers, security personnel, and lawyers. Their mission was to keep an eye on the keepers of secrets and stop these people from becoming the tellers of secrets. There was nothing illegal, immoral, or wrong with the general concept. Counterintelligence is an accepted practice.

Unfortunately, they were overzealous in the performance of their duties. Illegal "black bag jobs" (covert entry into private homes and offices) became an accepted methodology for gaining information. And the Plumbers' organization experienced what later came to be called "mission creep," where their realm of responsibilities expanded. The distinction between protecting official government secrets and secrets of the Nixon administration became blurred. Efforts to

prevent leaks expanded to efforts to obtain information regarding the lives and professional activities of a targeted group of individuals outside government (the "Enemies List").

Several members of the group (G. Gordon Liddy and E. Howard Hunt, most notably) were transferred from the White House payroll to that of the Committee to Reelect the President. The burglaries of the offices of the Democratic National Committee in the Watergate Complex were essentially Plumbers' operations.

The group was disbanded, of course, when revelations about the Watergate operations and the subsequent cover-up came to light. But the efforts to keep an eye on the keepers of secrets continue.

SECRETS SOLD: ROBERT HANSSEN

The FBI is charged with domestic counterintelligence activities. It is within the agency's charter to seek spies working for foreign governments and to provide specific information that would lead to arrest or expulsion. In addition to foreign spies, the FBI is in charge of keeping an eye on the secret-keepers within the government. As a practical matter, since there are so many secrets and so many secret-keepers spread throughout the government, most of the day-to-day activities are delegated to individual departments that work in close cooperation with the FBI.

As an agent employed by the FBI's counterintelligence unit, Robert Hanssen was in a unique position to know the methodologies employed by the Bureau in carrying out its tasks. He knew who was under investigation, where each investigation stood, the sources of information in each investigation, and the plans and objectives for the coming months.

No theoretician, Hanssen put his knowledge and expertise to practical use. Between 1979 and 2001, when he was finally caught, he collected $1.4 million in payments from the Soviet Union. During that period he was the most productive agent the Soviets had in place (that we know about, anyway).

He revealed the names of highly placed Soviet officials who were passing secrets to the Americans (at least four, three of whom are believed to have been executed). He revealed the existence of the tunnel that had been drilled as a listening post under the Soviet embassy in Washington, D.C. He passed along the contingency plans to be executed in case of a war with the Soviet Union. And he told the Soviets how the United States was able to monitor their diplomatic and military transmissions.

Hanssen's job was to keep an eye on the keepers of secrets to make sure they didn't become the tellers of secrets. To accomplish this, all he really had to do was look in the mirror.

When he was finally caught in 2001, he confessed to everything. In return for his cooperation, he was spared the death penalty but was instead sentenced to life imprisonment without the possibility of parole.

As part of the deal, his family receives an annual pension of $39,000 from the

Robert Hanssen

During the course of his counterespionage duties while with the Federal Bureau of Investigation, Hanssen was in the unique position of knowing that his activities as a spy for the Soviet Union were not causing undue suspicion to fall on him. (Federal Bureau of Investigation)

FBI. He is prohibited, by the terms of his sentencing deal, from writing or speaking about his illegal activities.

The exact sequence of events leading to his capture remains somewhat (purposely) obscure. His lifestyle was modest, although somewhat more upscale than would be expected with someone living on an FBI agent's salary; it drew comment but no undue attention. The fall of the Soviet Union led to the opening of the archives of the KGB (Soviet secret service), and information there may have led back to his office.

SECRETS YET TO BE REVEALED: *KRYPTOS*

The Berlin Wall was erected around the city of West Berlin in Germany in 1961. It came to be a symbol of the Cold War. By sheer coincidence, its construction coincided with the opening of the permanent headquarters building of the CIA in Langley, Virginia, just outside Washington, D.C.

The Berlin Wall fell in 1989, marking the end of the Cold War. By another coincidence, shortly after, in 1990, the CIA opened a second building on its campus. A piece of sculpture was commissioned to be placed outside the new headquarters building. This is a routine matter with all newly constructed federal buildings. The name of the sculpture is *Kryptos*. Taken from the Greek and meaning "hidden," the name is significant on a number of levels.

There is a covert aspect to our foreign intelligence service. They are in the business of secrets—finding them, hiding them, and telling them to the right people. The sculpture reflects this mission. It is made of materials native to American soil: wood, petrified wood, metal. It is in the shape of a scroll, almost as if it were a piece of paper flowing from a computer's printer. And imbedded in the metal scroll are four messages encrypted in code, each with its own encryption scheme.

The first three messages have been solved. The fourth is elusive.

But just to make things a little more interesting, it has been rumored that the "official" CIA transcript contains at least two typographic errors. It has also been rumored that the first two solutions require the use of the Vigenère table (see page 104).

The solutions are also a bit of a moving target, but not for lack of trying. People have devoted much time attempting to crack the secret and unleash the hidden message. As recently as April 2006, revisions to the official solutions have been issued. For the most recent information, tips and clues, visit this unofficial, but very detailed, site: http://elonka.com/kryptos/.

The artist, James Sanborn, remains enigmatic with regard to the piece and the progress toward solving the puzzle. He may occasionally offer an opinion but rarely an insight.

Should you wish to lend a hand in cracking the code, you are invited to get more information on the CIA's Web site (www.cia.gov). For the record, according to the CIA, the code is as follows on the next page.

THE *KRYPTOS* CODE

Left Side of Code

```
EMUFPHZLRFAXYUSDJKZLDKRNSHGNFIVJ
YQTQUXQBQVYUVLLTREVJYQTMKYRDMFD
VFPJUDEEHZWETZYVGWHKKQETGFQJNCE
GGWHKK?DQMCPFQZDQMMIAGPFXHQRLG
TIMVMZJANQLVKQEDAGDVFRPJUNGEUNA
QZGZLECGYUXUEENJTBJLBQCRTBJDFHRR
YIZETKZEMVDUFKSJHKFWHKUWQLSZFTI
HHDDUVH?DWKBFUFPWNTDFIYCUQZERE
EVLDKFEZMOQQJLTTUGSYQPFEUNLAVIDX
FLGGTEZ?FKZBSFDQVGOGIPUFXHHDRKF
FHQNTGPUAECNUVPDJMQCLQUMUNEDFQ
ELZZVRRGKFFVOEEXBDMVPNFQXEZLGRE
DNQFMPNZGLFLPMRJQYALMGNUVPDXVKP
DQUMEBEDMHDAFMJGZNUPLGEWJLLAETG
ENDYAHROHNLSRHEOCPTEOIBIDYSHNAIA
CHTNREYULDSLLSLLNOHSNOSMRWXMNE
TPRNGATIHNRARPESLNNELEBLPIIACAE
WMTWNDITEENRAHCTENEUDRETNHAEOE
TFOLSEDTIWENHAEIOYTEYQHEENCTAYCR
EIFTBRSPAMHNEWENATAMATEGYEERLB
TEEFOASFIOTUETUAEOTOARMAEERTNRTI
BSEDDNIAAHTTMSTEWPIEROAGRIEWFEB
AECTDDHILCEIHSITEGOEAOSDDRYDLORIT
RKLMLEHAGTDHARDPNEOHMGFMFEUHE
ECDMRIPFEIMEHNLSSTTRTVDOHW?OBKR
UOXOGHULBSOLIFBBWFLRVQQPRNGKSSO
TWTQSJQSSEKZZWATJKLUDIAWINFBNYP
VTTMZFPKWGDKZXTJCDIGKUHUAUEKCAR
```

Right Side of Code

```
A B C D E F G H I J K L M N O P Q R S T U V W X Y Z A B C D
A K R Y P T O S A B C D E F G H I J L M N Q U V W X Z K R Y P
B R Y P T O S A B C D E F G H I J L M N Q U V W X Z K R Y P T
C Y P T O S A B C D E F G H I J L M N Q U V W X Z K R Y P T O
D P T O S A B C D E F G H I J L M N Q U V W X Z K R Y P T O S
E T O S A B C D E F G H I J L M N Q U V W X Z K R Y P T O S A
F O S A B C D E F G H I J L M N Q U V W X Z K R Y P T O S A B
G S A B C D E F G H I J L M N Q U V W X Z K R Y P T O S A B C
H A B C D E F G H I J L M N Q U V W X Z K R Y P T O S A B C D
I B C D E F G H I J L M N Q U V W X Z K R Y P T O S A B C D E
J C D E F G H I J L M N Q U V W X Z K R Y P T O S A B C D E F
K D E F G H I J L M N Q U V W X Z K R Y P T O S A B C D E F G
L E F G H I J L M N Q U V W X Z K R Y P T O S A B C D E F G H
M F G H I J L M N Q U V W X Z K R Y P T O S A B C D E F G H I
N G H I J L M N Q U V W X Z K R Y P T O S A B C D E F G H I J
O H I J L M N Q U V W X Z K R Y P T O S A B C D E F G H I J L
P I J L M N Q U V W X Z K R Y P T O S A B C D E F G H I J L M
Q J L M N Q U V W X Z K R Y P T O S A B C D E F G H I J L M N
R L M N Q U V W X Z K R Y P T O S A B C D E F G H I J L M N Q
S M N Q U V W X Z K R Y P T O S A B C D E F G H I J L M N Q U
T N Q U V W X Z K R Y P T O S A B C D E F G H I J L M N Q U V
U Q U V W X Z K R Y P T O S A B C D E F G H I J L M N Q U V W
V U V W X Z K R Y P T O S A B C D E F G H I J L M N Q U V W X
W V W X Z K R Y P T O S A B C D E F G H I J L M N Q U V W X Z
X W X Z K R Y P T O S A B C D E F G H I J L M N Q U V W X Z K
Y X Z K R Y P T O S A B C D E F G H I J L M N Q U V W X Z K R
Z Z K R Y P T O S A B C D E F G H I J L M N Q U V W X Z K R Y
A B C D E F G H I J K L M N O P Q R S T U V W X Y Z A B C D
```

Kryptos

Public art that most of the public will never get to see is located in the courtyard of the campus of the new Central Intelligence Agency facility in Langley, Virginia, just outside Washington, D.C. The meaning of the code has yet to be successfully deciphered. (Central Intelligence Agency)

"Three may keep a secret," according to *Poor Richard's Almanac*, "if two of them are dead." There is wisdom here. The sage of Philadelphia, Benjamin Franklin, may have gotten it exactly right.

Codes and ciphers . . . broken. Druids and Hobos . . . revealed. Semaphore and invisible inks and secret writing . . . intercepted. Decoder badges and Enigma machines . . . cracked. Hieroglyphics and graffiti . . . translated. Spies of the Revolution and spies of the Cold War . . . busted. Microdots . . . enlarged. Easter Eggs . . . on the Internet. And the contents of clandestine taping systems . . . available for downloading.

The system and methodologies examined in the preceding pages have two fundamental things in common: (1) all have been attempts to transmit information in a covert manner, and (2) none have been successful in the long term. Perhaps there is a lesson here.

It may well be that the message Dr. Franklin was attempting to impart in 1735 holds true to the twenty-first century.

If you've got a secret, and you want to keep a secret, there is only one sure way how to tell a secret:

Don't.

BIBLIOGRAPHY

BOOKS

Beresniak, Daniel, *Symbols of Freemasonry.* New York: Assouline Publishing, 2000

Bucher, Lloyd M., and Mark Rascovich. *Bucher: My Story.* Garden City, NY: Doubleday, 1970

Butcher, Harry C. *My Three Years With Eisenhower.* New York: Simon & Schuster, 1946

Dulles, Allen, ed. *Great True Spy Stories.* New York: Harper & Row, 1968

Dunnigan, James F., and Albert A Nofi. *Dirty Little Secrets of World War II.* New York: William Morrow, 1994

Editors of *Time Magazine. Time Capsule: History of the War Years.* New York: Bonanza Books, 1967

Eisenschiml, Otto, and Ralph Newman. *The Civil War as We Lived It.* New York: Grosset & Dunlap, 1947

Farago, Ladislas. *The Broken Seal: "Operation Magic" and the Secret Road to Pearl Harbor.* New York: Random House, 1967

Green, Terisa. *The Tattoo Encyclopedia.* New York: Simon & Schuster, 2003

Haswell, Jock. *D-Day: Intelligence and Deception.* New York: Times Books, 1979

Hesketh, Roger. *Fortitude: The D-Day Deception Campaign.* New York: Overlook Press, 2002

Kahn, David. *The Codebreakers: The Story of Secret Writing.* New York: Macmillan, 1967

Kennett, Lee. *For the Duration: The United States Goes to War.* New York: Charles Scribner's Sons, 1985

Kozaczuk, Wladyslaw. *Enigma.* Bethesda, MD: University Publications of America, 1984

McCombs, Don, and Fred L. Worth. *World War II: 4,139 Strange and Fascinating Facts.* New York: Wing Books, 1983

Moore, Frank, ed. *The Civil War in Song and Story, 1860–1865.* New York: P.F. Collier, 1889

Myagkov, Aleksei. *Inside the KGB.* New Rochelle, NY: Arlington House, 1976

O'Toole, G.J.A. *Honorable Treachery.* New York: Atlantic Monthly Press, 1991

Peters, Harry T. *Currier & Ives: Printmakers to the American People.* Garden City, NY: Doubleday, Doran & Co., 1942

Peterson, Dick. *Louie, Louie: Me Gotta Go Now.* Bloomington, IN: AuthorHouse, 2006

Smith, Richard Furnald. *Prelude to Science: An Exploration of Magic and Divination.* New York: Charles Scribner's Sons, 1975

Tully, Jim. *Beggars of Life: A Hobo Autobiography.* New York: Albert & Charles Boni, 1925

Winterbotham, F.W. *The Ultra Secret.* New York: Harper & Row, 1974

Woodward, Bob. *The Secret Man: The Story of Watergate's Deep Throat.* New York: Simon & Schuster, 2005

Wrixon, Fred B. *Codes, Ciphers & Other Cryptic & Clandestine Communication.* New York: Barnes & Noble Books, 1998

WEB SITES

Americana and collectibles:
http://www.hakes.com/

The Central Intelligence Agency:
http://www.cia.gov/

Contemporary urban graffiti:
http://www.streetgangs.com/graffiti/

The Defense Intelligence Agency
http://www.dia.mil/

Easter eggs:
http://eeggs.com/
http://www.eggheaven2000.com/

The intelligence community:
http://www.intelligence.gov/index.shtml

The Manhattan Project:
http://www.atomicmuseum.com/tour/manhattanproject.cfm

MIS-X:
http://www.aiipowmia.com/wwii/msx.html

The National Reconnaissance Office:
http://www.nro.gov/

The National Security Agency:
http://www.nsa.gov/

Passwords:
http://www.modernlifeisrubbish.co.uk/top-10-most-common-passwords.asp

Presidential tapes:
http://www.whitehousetapes.org/

Sealand:
http://www.sealandgov.org/

Tattoos, contemporary and historic:
http://www.tattooarchive.com/

Video surveillance:
http://www.observingsurveillance.org/

Writing and Graffiti from Pompeii:
http://www.jact.org/subjects/latinresources.htm

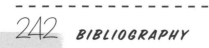

ACKNOWLEDGMENTS

A WORK LIKE THIS DOES NOT SPRING INTO BEING OF ITS OWN ACcord. The authors are grateful to friends and family who offered encouragement and suggestions along the way.

In addition to the books, periodicals, libraries, and archives consulted during the course of research, we were fortunate to encounter a number of people who were generous with their time and patient with their response to questioning. In large measure, it is the expertise and guidance they shared that allowed us to produce this book. We refer to Dr. David Hatch, historian with the National Cryptologic Museum for background, insight, and pointers; to Patrick Gleason and Brian St. Pierre of the Baltimore Ravens and to Bien Figueroa and Ryan Sakamoto of the Frederick Keys for deep background into the goings-on on a professional sports field (with sincere hopes that we didn't give too much away); to Dick Peterson of the Kingsmen, once a hero and now a friend, for the real story of "Louie, Louie"; to Gabriel Moore of Skin Script Tattoos of York, Pennsylvania, and C.W. Eldridge of the Tattoo Archive for a fresh look at skin art; to D.H. Lewin for an appreciation of Tom Mix (one more thing on a long list owed to the man); to Ted Hake of Hake's Americana and Collectibles, for his encyclopedic knowledge of American popular culture; to Dr. Lillian Schwartz for her views of Leonardo; and to Michael J. Kazin for all things digital.

This book never would have been written if Ellen Nanney of the Smithsonian Institution hadn't seen the potential, or if Donna Sanzone of HarperCollins hadn't believed.

And if Lisa Hacken and Stephanie Meyers of the Editorial Group of Harper-Collins hadn't been willing to wrestle with the text and decipher the authors' musings, it all would have come to naught. Truly we are grateful for their adherence to deadlines, their skill with recalcitrant authors, and their expertise with poorly worded phrases and not-quite-complete-but-submitted-nonetheless thoughts. We stand in awe of their prowess.

All these people deserve credit. Any errors belong to the authors alone.

INDEX

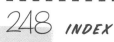

PICTURE CREDITS

The authors wish to gratefully acknowledge the people, organizations, and archives for the use of the images that appear in this book:

Dick Peterson—Chapter 5: "The Kingsmen"

Dr. Lillian Schwartz—Chapter 5: "Leonardo's Real Secret?"

Air America.org—Chapter 6: "Air America"

The American Playing Card Company—Chapter 5: "MIS-X"

The Baltimore Ravens—Chapter 3: "Brian St. Pierre"

Corbis Images—Chapter 5: "The Hawaiian Good Luck Sign"; Chapter 6: "President Franklin D. Roosevelt," "German Rear Admiral Wilhelm Canaris," "The Fall of Saigon, Vietnam"

Hake's Americana and Collectibles—Chapter 1: "The Lone Ranger's Secret Victory Code"; Chapter 2: "Roosevelt Rebus," "Currier & Ives Rebus"; Chapter 3: "Little Orphan Annie Hand Signals"

Kismet Images—Chapter 1: "Victory from the World War II Homefront"; Chapter 2: "Ideogram," "Logogram," "The Rosetta Stone," "When Secrecy Was More Important Than Speed," "Ogham"; Chapter 3: "Semaphore," "WWI Comic Postcard," "Tom Mix Images," "Twentieth-Century American Pictoglyph," "Warchalking," "Street Gang Graffiti," "Keyote";

Chapter 4: "Skytale," "Vigenère Table," Chapter 4: "Remember the Pueblo," "Louie, Louie," "Camoflauge," "Messages On the Wing," "Signal Corps Message Book"; Chapter 6: "Civil War Intelligence," "Extra Security"; Chapter 7: "World War II Occupation Currency," "Greater East Asia Co-Prosperity Sphere"

NBCU Photo Bank—Chapter 1: "Don't Be Silly"

Photri/Microstock Image—Chapter 2: "American Pictoglyph," "Rune Stone," "Windtalkers"

Tattoo Archive—Chapter 3: "Charlie Wagner"

The Arlington Room of the Arlington (VA) County Public Library—Chapter 1: "Tapping the Lines"

The William L. Clements Library of the University of Michigan—Chapter 4: "Secret Writing During the Revolution"

The Central Intelligence Agency—Chapter 7: "Kryptos"

The Federal Bureau of Investigation—Chapter 7: "Deep Throat," "Robert Hanssen"

The Library of Congress—Introduction: "Can You Keep a Secret?"; Chapter 1: "Winston Churchill"; Chapter 2: "Doctor Franklin's Rebus"; Chapter 3: "Which Way 'Bo?"; Chapter 4: "John Wilkes Booth"; Chapter 5: "Censored"; Chapter 6: "Steven Grover Cleveland," "President John F. Kennedy"; Chapter 7: "General Robert E. Lee, CSA," "General George McClellan, USA," "Watch Meeting," "Looking for Secrets"

The National Archives and Records Administraton—Chapter 1: General Dwight David Eisenhower"; Chapter 2: "Smoke Signals"; Chapter 3: "Semaphore Station," "Plains War Semaphore"; Chapter 4: "Winston Churchill," "Patton," "Confederate Cipher Machine," "The Purple Machine"; Chapter 5: "The USS. *Pueblo*," "Crew of the USS. *Pueblo*," "Monty," "Monty's Double"; Chapter 6: "Edmund Randolph," "General James Wilkerson," "The Soviet Union's TU-4," "The American U2," "Pearl Harbor"; Chapter 7: "Herbert O. Yardley," "The Battle of Midway," "Nixon and Staff"

The National Cryptologic Museum—Chapter 1: "The Bombe"; Chapter 3: "Slave Quilt"; Chapter 4: "A Gift," "Jefferson's Cipher Machine," "Enigma," "Enigma in the Field," "Winston Churchill"; Chapter 7: "Lieutenant Commander Joseph Rochefort"

The United States Air Force—Chapter 5: "He's Counting on You"

The United States Department of Energy—Chapter 4: "The Supercomputer"; Chapter 6: "The Atomic Age," "Hiroshima"

The United States Department of Transportation—Chapter 6: "BIGOT-in Chief"
